First Published In 2021 By Charles Phillips

CONTENTS

INTRODUCTION

Cooking on a charcoal grill can be slightly more complicated than using a gas or electric grill, especially if you're new to the game. But we've got you covered! Here are our eight top tips to help you master the art of charcoal grilling.

8 Tips to Help You Master Your Charcoal Grill

Use a Chimney Starter

Chimney starters are a must for charcoal grilling. They will light up to 100 charcoal briquets and get them red hot within 20 minutes, using nothing but a match and a single sheet of newspaper. No more lighter fluid! That means no more exploding lighter fluid or food that tastes like kerosene.

The best chimney starters are the 6-quart models, and you can find them at hardware stores and home stores everywhere.

Use the Right Amount of Charcoal

Once you've gotten your hands on a chimney starter and you're comfortable using it, everything else seems to fall into place. Especially the question of how much charcoal to use. Your target grill temperatures can be easily reckoned in terms of how full your chimney is.

For high-heat grilling, (450 to 550 F, which is ideal for grilling steaks and thin cuts of meat), you want a full chimney. For medium heat (350 to 450 F, perfect for chicken pieces, veggies and seafood), 1/2 to 3/4 chimney. And for low heat (250 to 350 F, for grilling pork ribs, whole poultry, larger roasts and smoking), 1/4 chimney.

Oil and Preheat the Cooking Grate

Oiling the cooking grate ensures that your food doesn't stick to the grill. Preheating is just as important. Trying to cook a steak on a cold grill will cause it to spend too long on the grill and overcook. You also won't get those lovely grill marks. For safety, oil the grate before you set it over the hot coals. Here's more about taking care of your charcoal grill.

Learn How to Vent

Unlike with a gas grill (or your kitchen range), you can't adjust the temperature with a knob or dial on a charcoal grill. But you can control how hot the coals on your grill burn by controlling the flow of oxygen, and you do that by opening and closing the vents.

Opening the vents allows more oxygen, which produces a hotter grill. Trimming the vents slows the oxygen, which cools the grill. But don't close them all the way or your fire will suffocate. And make sure your grill isn't full of ash, which can obstruct the vents.

Know the Difference Between Direct vs Indirect Heat

Another way of controlling how quickly your food cooks is by understanding the difference between direct and indirect heat. A certain amount of coals will produce a certain temperature, but your food will cook faster if it is situated directly above those coals as opposed to away from them. This fact leads us to our next tip...

Build a Two-Zone Fire

Once you've mastered this technique, you're well on your way to mastering charcoal grilling. It's simply a matter of loading the charcoal onto one side of the grill and leaving the other side empty.

It'll still be hot on that side, but it will enable you to move items from the hot, direct-heat side, to the cooler, indirect-heat side. The cooler zone will help prevent overcooking and scorching and will allow you, for example, to grill vegetables and steaks at the same time.

Deal With Flare-ups

A two-zone fire will also help you deal with flare-ups caused by fat from a steak or burger dripping onto the coals. Instead of controling flare-ups using a spray bottle, which can blow ash onto your food, simply move the dripping item over to the indirect zone. With no coals directly underneath, the dripping fat won't flare up.

Enhance Flavor with Wood

The last step on your way to becoming a master of charcoal grilling is incorporating wood. Whether you're doing a full smoke or a true low-temperature barbecue, or you simply want to add some smoke flavor to your grilled items, wood is the key.

Hickory, mesquite, and fruitwoods like apple and cherry, are grillmaster favorites. For smoking and barbecuing, use chunks of dried wood. But for grilling, you can simply add some wood chips on top of your hot coals. Be sure to soak the wood chips first.

FISH AND SEAFOOD

Honey Glazed Smoked Halibut

Servings:8
Cooking Time: 150 Minutes

Ingredients:

- 6 oz halibut filets
- Meat Church Honey Hog or Deez Nuts Honey Pecan rub
- 4 tbsp clover honey
- 1/2 C kosher salt
- 1 C sugar
- 4 tbsp cumin
- 1 tbsp white pepper
- 2 bay leaves crushed
- 1/2 gallon water

Directions:

1. Preheat the grill to 275°F using direct heat with a cast iron grate installed. We recommend lighter smoking wood for this smoke. Alder wood, fruit wood or pecan will pair nicely with a white fish while not being too overpowering.
2. Prepare the Brine Mix all brine ingredients in water and dissolve thoroughly. Pour the brine over the filets and let them sit for two hours. It's ok if the fish floats.
3. Prepare the Halibut. After 2 hours remove the fish from the brine, rinse off and pat dry.
4. Season with Meat Church Honey Hog or Deez Nuts Honey Pecan rub on all sides.
5. This is optional, but if you prefer a bolder flavor profile, try adding some cracked pepper over the top of the halibut after you have seasoned with the rub.
6. Place the filets directly on the cooking grate skin side down. The skin will act as a barrier to the heat and come off easily after the cook. Smoke the fish until it reaches an internal temperature of 135°F degrees. This smoke will take around 30 minutes at 275°F.
7. Optional Glaze Drizzle the filet with warm honey the last 10 minutes of the cook for nice and simple honey glaze. Honey can also be mixed 50 with miso to create a miso-honey glaze.
8. Remove the fish carefully with a spatula. Place it on a plate to rest for 10 minutes. Eat and enjoy!

Clam Bake

Servings: 6
Cooking Time: 30 Minutes

Ingredients:

- 2 lbs mussels, scrubbed and debearded
- 1 1/2 lbs kielbasa sausage, sliced into 1 inch chunks
- 1 1/2 lbs small potatoes (we like red potatoes)
- 2 large onions, roughly chopped
- 2 dozen littleneck clams, scrubbed
- 2 dozen steamer clams, scrubbed
- 2 cups dry white wine
- 2 Tablespoons olive oil
- 1 Tablespoon salt
- 1/2 Tablespoon black pepper

Directions:

1. Preheat the grill to 350°F using direct heat with a cast iron grate installed with the dutch oven on the grid.
2. Add olive oil and onion to the pot and cook until soft, about 5 minutes.
3. Add ingredients in layers in the following order: Kielbasa, Potatoes, Clams, Mussels.
4. Pour in the white wine and cover.
5. Lower the dome for 15-20 minutes or until the potatoes are cooked through and the shellfish have opened up.
6. Ladle out the sausage, potatoes, and seafood and strain the broth, taking care not to get any sand from the clams.
7. Serve on sheets of parchment paper with broth in small bowls for dipping and sipping.
8. If you have never tried parsnips before, they look like a white carrot and taste like a cross between a carrot and horseradish. When they are braised they become sweet, a perfect alternative to plain carrots.

Shrimp Burgers With Remoulade

Servings: 4
Cooking Time: 10 Minutes

Ingredients:

- 1 lb raw shrimp, peeled & deveined
- 3/4 cups fresh breadcrumbs
- 1/4 cup celery, finely diced
- 1/4 cup green onion, white and light green parts, chopped
- 1/4 cup parsley
- 1 Tablespoon Old Bay Seasoning
- 1 Tablespoon brown mustard
- The juice and zest of 1 lemon
- Olive Oil for brushing
- 1/2 cup mayonnaise
- 2 Tablespoon dill pickle, finely chopped
- 2 tsp prepared horseradish
- 4 hamburger buns
- Shredded lettuce
- Sliced tomato

Directions:

1. In a food processor, combine burger ingredients, minus the breadcrumbs, and process until smooth. Gently fold in breadcrumbs and form into 4 patties. Refrigerate for 20 minutes.
2. Mix remoulade sauce ingredients and refrigerate.
3. Grilling:
4. Preheat the grill to 500°F using direct heat with a cast iron grate installed.
5. Brush both sides of the burgers with olive oil and place directly on the grids. Cover with the dome for 4 minutes.
6. Turn the burgers and cover for another 3 minutes.
7. Close all of the vents and allow the burgers to sit for another 5 minutes or until the burgers reach an internal temperature of 165°F.
8. Place the burgers on bottom buns and top with a dollop of remoulade, sliced tomato, and shredded lettuce.

Watermelon Pizza

Servings:2
Cooking Time: 12 Minutes

Ingredients:

- 1 Large Watermelon
- 12 Large Shrimp, peeled and deveined
- Sweet & Smoky Seasoning
- 3 TBS olive oil
- 1 cup tomatoes, diced
- 1 Jalapeño, sliced
- 10 sprigs of Cilantro, chopped
- 1 cup of Feta cheese, crumbled
- 4 Bamboo Skewers, soaked
- Salt to taste

Directions:

1. Preheat the grill to 400°F using direct heat with a cast iron grate installed.
2. Skewer the shrimp and season with the olive oil and Sweet & Smoky Seasoning.
3. Cut the Watermelon in a 3-inch diameter. Lightly salt the watermelon.
4. Grill Watermelon 3 minutes on each side and remove from the grill.
5. Grill the shrimp 3 minutes per side and remove from the grill.
6. Build the pizza with the shrimp, feta cheese, jalapeño, tomatoes and cilantro. Grill for another 5 minutes to soften feta and watermelon.
7. Enjoy!

Grilled Fish Tacos

Servings:10
Cooking Time: 5minutes

Ingredients:

- 1 teaspoon cumin
- 1 teaspoon brown sugar
- 1 teaspoon ground coriander
- 2 teaspoons olive oil
- 1½ pounds fresh salmon, halibut, catfish, or your favorite fish
- Corn tortillas
- Lime wedges
- 1½ cups diced fresh peaches
- 1 firm, but ripe avocado, diced
- ¼ cup thinly sliced red onion
- 2 tablespoons chopped fresh cilantro
- ½ small jalapeño, minced
- juice of 1 lime, about 3 tablespoons

Directions:

1. Preheat the grill to 400°F using direct heat with a cast iron grate installed.
2. In a small bowl, combine cumin, sugar, and coriander. Brush fish with olive oil and sprinkle with spice mixture. Grill fish on oiled cooking grid for 3-5 minutes per side until cooked to your liking. Char tortillas on cooking grid, about 10 seconds on each side.
3. Serve tacos with fresh salsa and desired toppings. (cheese, etc.)
4. Combine salsa ingredients in a medium bowl and refrigerate until ready to use.

Grilled Shrimp Cocktail With Fire-roasted Cocktail Sauce

Servings:4
Cooking Time: 35 Minutes

Ingredients:

- 1 tablespoon olive oil
- 1⁄2 teaspoon Garlic Salt
- 16 jumbo shrimp (about 1 pound), peeled and deveined 1 cup Fire-Roasted Cocktail Sauce
- 1 tablespoon chopped flat-leaf (Italian) parsley
- 1 lemon, cut into 4 wedges or 8 slices
- 1 cup canned no-salt-added fire-roasted diced tomatoes
- 1 tablespoon horseradish
- 1 tablespoon lime juice
- 1⁄4 teaspoon Chipotle Puree (optional)

Directions:

1. Preheat the grill to 350°F using direct heat with a cast iron grate installed.
2. Combine the oil and garlic salt in a medium bowl. Add the shrimp and toss well.
3. Skewer the shrimp, place the shrimp on the cooking grid and cook for about 3 minutes on each side, or until pink and firm. Remove from the heat.
4. Spoon 1⁄4 cup of cocktail sauce into each of 4 decorative glasses. Top with 4 shrimp per glass. Sprinkle with the parsley and garnish with the lemon wedges or slices.
5. Combine all the ingredients in a blender or food processor and puree until smooth. Transfer the sauce to a jar and chill for at least 30 minutes before using to let the flavors meld. The sauce will keep in the refrigerator for about 1 month.

Shrimp & Cheddar Tostada

Servings:6
Cooking Time: 10 Minutes

Ingredients:

- ¼ cup fat free cream cheese, softened
- ¼ cup reduced-fat mayonnaise
- 2 tablespoons skim milk
- ¼ cup finely chopped fresh cilantro
- 2 tablespoons fresh lime juice, divided
- 30 medium-size shrimp, peeled and deveined (about 1 pound)
- 2 tablespoons barbecue rub or seasoning
- ½ teaspoon salt
- Cooking spray
- 6 (6-inch) corn tortillas
- 4 ounces Cabot Jalapeno Light Cheddar or Cabot Sharp Light Cheddar, grated (about 1 cup)
- 6 tablespoons finely chopped fresh tomato

Directions:

1. In small bowl, combine cream cheese, mayonnaise and milk; whisk until smooth. Stir in cilantro and 1 tablespoon of lime juice. Cover and refrigerate until serving time.
2. When ready to serve, thread 5 shrimp onto flexible skewers. In small bowl, combine barbecue rub and salt. Brush shrimp with remaining 1 tablespoon lime juice and dredge in rub mixture. Place kabobs in shallow dish; cover and refrigerate for 15 minutes.
3. Preheat the grill to 350°F using direct heat with a cast iron grate installed.
4. Place kabobs on kamado grill grid coated with cooking spray and cook for 3 minutes on each side, or until done. Set aside.
5. Place tortillas directly on kamado grill and cook for 4 minutes. Top each tortilla with some of cheese and bake until cheese is melted, about 3 minutes longer.
6. Place 1 tortilla on each of 6 individual serving plates. Top each with 5 grilled shrimp and 2 tablespoons cilantro mayonnaise. Sprinkle with tomato and serve.

Chicken And Shrimp Paella

Servings:6
Cooking Time: 30 Minutes

Ingredients:

- 15 large shrimp (feel free to add clams or mussels)
- 1 lb (450 g) chicken thighs
- 8 cups (1.9 L) chicken stock
- 1 pinch saffron
- ½ cup (120 ml) fresh parsley
- 2 to 3 tbsp (30 to 45 ml) fresh thyme
- 8 oz (225 g) chorizo sausages, sliced bite-size
- 3 garlic cloves, minced
- 1 large onion, diced
- 1 large bell pepper, diced
- 4 plum tomatoes, diced
- 4 tbsp (60 ml) tomato paste
- ½ tbsp (8 ml) paprika
- 1 cup (240 ml) olives, pitted and diced
- 3 cups (710 ml) calasparra rice
- 3 lemons, quartered

Directions:

1. Preheat the grill to 500°F using direct heat with a cast iron grate installed.
2. Peel shrimp, leaving on the tail. Lightly salt the chicken thighs and shrimp. Heat the chicken stock with saffron and herbs; keep hot but not boiling as you cook.
3. Coat the bottom of a Stir-Fry & Paella Pan with olive oil. Add the pan to the cooking grid and brown the chorizo for 1 or 2 minutes; set aside. Brown the chicken for 2 to 3 minutes; set aside.
4. Sauté garlic, onion and bell pepper until softened, adding tomatoes shortly before the mixture is finished. Add the tomato paste, paprika and olives; stir in the chicken and chorizo. Add rice, mixing together and stirring one minute. When the rice is slightly translucent add enough chicken stock to cover the whole mixture and lower the kamado grill temperature to 375°F.
5. Stir a few times in the first 10 minutes, adding broth as necessary to keep the rice fully covered. After this let the paella sit and cook another 10-20 minutes, adding broth bit by bit to keep the rice submerged until the rice on the top is al dente. Stir the paella one last time and place the shrimp on top, turning over after 2 to 4 minutes to cook on the other side. Carefully remove the paella from the kamado grill, cover and let rest for 15-20 minutes. Garnish with lemon wedges.

Miso Poached Sea Bass

Servings: 4
Cooking Time: 55 Minutes

Ingredients:

- 4 large eggs
- 3 tbsp white miso paste
- 4 sea bass fillets, about 6oz (170g) each, skinned and deboned
- 3 medium red-skinned potatoes
- 12 fresh green beans
- 1 red onion
- 1 medium head of butter lettuce
- 2 large beefsteak tomatoes, sliced
- 16 Kalamata olives, pitted
- 4 tbsp capers
- 2 tbsp chopped fresh flat-leaf parsley
- for the dressing
- 4 garlic cloves, crushed
- 2 tsp Dijon mustard
- 6 tbsp extra virgin olive oil
- 2 tbsp soy sauce
- 2 tbsp white miso
- 3 tbsp rice vinegar
- kosher salt and freshly ground black pepper
- to smoke
- grapevine or apple wood chunks

Directions:

1. Place eggs in a medium saucepan and cover with cold water. Cover the pot with a lid and bring to a boil on the stovetop over high heat. Once boiling, remove the pot from the heat, keep it covered, and let sit for 20 minutes. Drain the water, and set eggs aside to cool. Once cool, peel, halve, and refrigerate until ready to use.
2. To make the dressing, in a small bowl, whisk together garlic, Dijon mustard, oil, soy sauce, miso, and rice vinegar. Season with salt and pepper to taste, and set aside.
3. Preheat the grill to 425°F (218°C) using direct heat with a cast iron grate installed. Add enough water in the dutch oven to cover bass. (Don't add bass to the water yet.) Place the dutch oven on the grate, leave the lid off the dutch oven, and close the grill lid.
4. Once the water starts to simmer, place the wood chunks on the coals. Add miso paste, stirring to dissolve, and then add fish fillets. Leave the lid off the dutch oven, close the grill lid, and cook until cooked through, about 10 minutes per inch of thickness. Remove from the water and set aside.
5. Place potatoes, green beans, and onion on the grate around the dutch oven. Close the lid and grill until charred, about 7 to 10 minutes. Remove the vegetables from the grill, and chop potatoes and onion. Place the vegetables in a medium bowl, add the dressing, and stir to coat.
6. Line a serving platter with the large outer lettuce leaves. Chop the remainder and arrange on the platter. Place tomato slices on one end of the platter, followed by the grilled vegetables. (Don't throw out the dressing from the bowl.) Place fish in the center of the platter. Garnish with sliced hard-boiled eggs, olives, and capers. Sprinkle parsley over top and drizzle the remaining dressing before serving.

Shrimp Tacos

Servings:6
Cooking Time: 33 Minutes

Ingredients:

- 1 lbs of shrimp, peeled and deveined
- 1 cup tomatoes, diced
- 5-6 skewers, soaked
- 3 Tbsp olive oil
- Sweet & Smoky Seasoning
- 4-5 Flour or Corn tortillas
- Vinaigrette Slaw
- Avocado Spread
- 4 cups cabbage
- ¼ cup of apple cider vinegar
- ¼ cup of olive oil
- 2 Tbsp of sugar
- 1 jalapeño, diced
- 1/3 cup of white onion
- 10 sprigs of cilantro, chopped
- Salt to taste
- Pepper to taste
- 1 large avocado
- 1 cup sour cream
- 1 tsp of lime, freshly squeezed
- Salt to taste

Directions:

1. Preheat the grill to 400°F using direct heat with a cast iron grate installed.
2. Skewer the shrimp, drizzle with olive oil and season with Sweet & Smoky Seasoning. Grill 3 minutes on each side.
3. Remove the shrimp from the grill. Construct tacos with slaw, avocado spread and shrimp.
4. Mix all the slaw ingredients together and refrigerate for about 30 minutes.
5. Smash the avocado to preferred consistency. Mix all the ingredients together and set aside.

Black Pepper Dungeness Crab

Servings: 4
Cooking Time: 10 Minutes

Ingredients:

- 4 lbs Dungeness Crab
- 3 Tablespoons Hoisin sauce
- 3 Tablespoons Oyster sauce
- 2 Tablespoons butter
- 2 Tablespoons olive oil
- 2 Tablespoons freshly grated ginger
- 2 Tablespoons freshly cracked black pepper
- 2 Tablespoons red chile flakes
- 6 garlic cloves, finely chopped
- 2 green onions, finely chopped

Directions:

1. In a small sauce pan, heat butter and olive oil.
2. Add onions, garlic, ginger, pepper, and chile flakes and cook for 1 minute.
3. Add hoisin and oyster sauces and stir to warm. Keep warm over very low heat.
4. Grilling:
5. Preheat the grill to 500°F using direct heat with a cast iron grate installed.
6. Place the crabs on the grid and close the dome for 10 minutes or until the shells turn bright pink.
7. Remove the crabs from the grid and, using heat-proof gloves, quarter the crabs and slightly crack the legs.
8. Stir together half of the crabs and half of the warm sauce. Place on a platter.
9. Continue with the remaining crabs and remaining sauce. Serve

Whole Grilled Snapper In Pipian Sauce

Servings:10
Cooking Time: 76 Minutes

Ingredients:

- 2 whole snappers, cleaned, preferably with heads-on, each about 2 pounds
- Coarse salt, kosher or sea
- Freshly ground black pepper
- Lime, halved, for serving
- 1 sweet onion, peeled and thinly sliced
- 2 garlic cloves, peeled and thinly sliced
- 6 sprigs fresh cilantro
- 1 poblano chile (green or red), seeded and thinly sliced
- Extra virgin olive oil
- 8 fresh tomatillos, husked and rinsed
- 1 poblano pepper
- 3 serrano chiles
- ½ small onion
- 4 cloves garlic, peeled and skewered on a toothpick
- 2 scallions, trimmed
- 2 romaine lettuce leaves, cut into 1-inch slices
- 1 cup hulled pumpkin seeds
- ½ cup fresh cilantro, coarsely chopped
- 2 tbsp fresh flat-leaf parsley, coarsely chopped
- ½ tsp ground cumin
- 1 tbsp fresh lime juice, or more to taste
- 1 ½ cup water, or more as needed
- 2 tbsp extra virgin olive oil
- Sea salt and freshly ground black pepper to taste

Directions:

1. Preheat the grill to 450°F using direct heat with a cast iron grate installed.
2. Generously season the cavities of the fish with salt and pepper, then stuff with the onion, garlic, cilantro, and chile. Pin the cavities shut with toothpicks.
3. Brush the outside of the fish with olive oil, then make three diagonal, parallel slashes on the top side of each to facilitate even cooking.
4. Arrange the stuffed fish on the grill grate, slashed sides up.
5. Grill the fish until it is tender and the internal temperature is at least 145°F, 30 to 40 minutes, or as needed. Carefully transfer the fish to a platter using a wide spatula.
6. Preheat the grill to 500°F using direct heat with a cast iron grate installed.
7. Brush and oil the grill grate. Grill the tomatillos, poblano, serranos, onion, garlic, scallions, and lettuce leaves until golden brown, 2 to 4 minutes per side. Transfer to cutting board to cool to room temperature, then cut into 1-inch pieces.
8. Toast the pumpkin seeds in a dry cast iron skillet (not nonstick) over medium heat until they begin to brown and pop, 3 minutes. Shake the pan as the seeds cook; do not let them burn. Transfer the seeds to a shallow bowl to cool.
9. Set 3 tablespoons of seeds aside for a garnish, then grind the remaining seeds to a fine powder in a food processor, running the machine in short bursts. Work in 1/2 cup of water.
10. Place the grilled vegetables in a food processor and puree. Work in the cilantro, parsley, cumin, and lime juice. Work in an additional 1 cup water, adding more as needed to obtain a thick but pourable sauce.
11. Heat the olive oil in a large, deep skillet over medium heat. Add the pumpkin seed mixture and cook until dark, thick, and fragrant, about 5 minutes, stirring frequently to prevent splattering or scorching.
12. Stir in the tomatillo mixture and continue cooking the sauce until thick and richly flavored, 15 to 20 minutes, stirring often. Remove the sauce from the heat and taste for seasoning, adding salt to taste and/or more lime juice; the sauce should be highly seasoned. Set the sauce aside and keep it warm.
13. Spoon the Pipian Sauce over or under the fish. Sprinkle with the pumpkin seeds reserved from the sauce recipe. Serve with grilled limes halves for squeezing.

Grilled Rockefeller Oysters

Servings:12
Cooking Time: 5 Minutes

Ingredients:

- 12 shucked oysters
- 1⁄4 cup butter
- 1⁄2 cup red onions (chopped)
- 4 cloves garlic
- 1⁄2 cup Pinot Grigio
- 21⁄2 cups spinach (roughly chopped)
- 2 tbsp heavy cream
- 2 tbsp clam juice
- 1⁄2 cup mozzarella
- 2 tbsp crunchy bacon (chopped finely)

Directions:

1. Preheat the grill to 375°F using direct heat with a cast iron grate installed.
2. In a Stir-Fry and Paella Pan or other grill-safe pan, sauté onions in 2 tbsp butter on medium high until slightly translucent. Add Pinot Grigio and simmer for 2 minutes. Add the rest of the butter and garlic and cook for 1 minute. Add spinach and cook until spinach is wilted, and then add the heavy cream and clam juice and cook for a few more seconds.
3. Top oysters with spinach mixture and mozzarella and place on a Perforated Cooking Grid or directly on the cooking grid for about 5 minutes or until the cheese bubbles. Sprinkle with bacon and enjoy!

Southwest Baked Oysters

Servings:2
Cooking Time: 15 Minutes

Ingredients:

- Clean oyster shells
- Olive oil
- Oysters
- Finely chopped jalapeno chiles
- Shredded cheddar cheese or grated parmesan cheese
- Bacon bits or soy bacon bits
- Italian-style seasoned bread crumbs

Directions:

1. Preheat the grill to 375°F using direct heat with a cast iron grate installed.
2. Arrange they oyster shells in a Perforated Cooking Grid. Spray with olive oil. Place 1 large or 2 small oysters in each shell. Top each with 2 or 3 tiny pieces of jalapeno. Sprinkle with cheese and bacon bits. Top with bread crumbs.
3. Place pan on the cooking grid and bake at 375° for 10 to 15 minutes or until bubbly; do not overcook.

POULTRY

Bacon Wrapped Jalapeño Stuffed Chicken Thighs

Servings:6
Cooking Time: 30 Minutes

Ingredients:

- 8 boneless, skinless chicken thighs
- 4 jalapeño peppers
- 8 oz cream cheese
- 16 strips of bacon
- 1 stick of butter
- All-Purpose Rub
- Sweet and Smoky seasoning
- 1 cup salt
- 1/2 cup granulated garlic
- 1/4 cup black pepper

Directions:

1. Preheat the grill to 375°F using direct heat with a cast iron grate installed. If desired, add some pecan chips for some extra smokiness.
2. Remove the thighs from the packaging and place on a cutting board designated for poultry. Trim any excess fat on the thighs and season each side with a hefty dose of Sweet and Smoky seasoning.
3. Cut the jalapeño peppers in half lengthwise and remove the seeds and veins. Fill each half with cream cheese and sprinkle a touch of all-purpose rub on top.
4. Place the stuffed jalapeño peppers cheese side down in the center of each chicken thigh and form the meat around the pepper. Next, wrap each thigh with 2 strips of bacon.
5. Place the wrapped chicken thigh in a Drip Pan, and top each piece of chicken with a pat of butter. Cook for 30 minutes, until chicken reaches an internal temperature of 165°F.
6. Remove from the kamado grill and let the chicken rest for 8-10 minutes, sprinkle more Sweet and Smoky seasoning on the chicken and spoon some of the butter sauce over the chicken.
7. Serve immediately.
8. Mix all the ingredients together and set aside.

Rosemary Ranch Chicken Kebabs

Servings:4
Cooking Time: 12 Minutes

Ingredients:

- ½ cup olive oil
- ½ cup ranch dressing
- 3 Tbsp Worcestershire sauce
- 1 Tbsp minced fresh rosemary
- 2 tsp salt
- 1 tsp lemon juice
- 1 tsp white vinegar
- ¼ tsp ground black pepper, or to taste
- 1 Tbsp white sugar, or to taste (optional)
- 5 skinless, boneless chicken breast halves – cut into 1 inch cubes

Directions:

1. Preheat the grill to 400°F using direct heat with a cast iron grate installed.
2. In a medium bowl, stir together the olive oil, ranch dressing, Worcestershire sauce, rosemary, salt, lemon juice, white vinegar, pepper and sugar. Let stand for 5 minutes.
3. Add the chicken to the bowl and stir to coat with the marinade. Cover and refrigerate for 30 minutes. Thread chicken onto skewers and discard marinade.
4. Lightly oil the cooking grid. Grill skewers for 8 to 12 minutes, or until the chicken is no longer pink in the center, and the juices run clear.
5. Serve with grilled corn on the cob and grilled veggie skewers.

Butter-injected Turkey And Sides

Servings:16
Cooking Time: 350 Minutes

Ingredients:

- 1 12-14 lb. whole turkey
- 5 oz. Roasted Garlic & Herb Banner Butter, melted
- 1 orange, cut into wedges
- 1 sweet onion, cut into wedges
- 1 lemon, cut into wedges
- 2 whole heads of garlic, top cut off
- 3 sprigs rosemary
- 3 sprigs thyme
- 3 sprigs sage
- Savory Pecan Seasoning
- Extra virgin olive oil or canola oil
- Kosher salt
- 6 whole carrots
- ½ lb. red potatoes cut in half
- 8 oz whole baby Portobello mushrooms
- 2 zucchinis, cut into ½ inch strips
- 8 oz cherry tomatoes
- 8 oz green beans
- 5 oz. Fig & Balsamic Banner Butter, melted
- 2 tbsp extra virgin olive oil
- ½ tbsp kosher salt
- ¼ tbsp cracked black pepper
- 2 tbsp Worcestershire sauce
- 4 sweet potatoes
- 2 tbsp brown sugar
- ½ tbsp kosher salt
- ½ cup butter

Directions:

1. Preheat the grill to 350°F using direct heat with a cast iron grate installed.
2. Pat the turkey dry and coat with oil, season with salt and Savory Pecan Seasoning. Pull melted butter into the injector and evenly inject the turkey with the butter (to prevent splash back from the injector, cover the turkey with plastic wrap and inject the turkey through the plastic wrap.)
3. Place half of the onion, one whole head of garlic, half the orange, half the lemon, and two sprigs of each herb inside the cavity of the turkey. Fold the wings back behind the turkey so that they cook evenly. Add the remaining garlic, onion, orange, lemon and herbs around the turkey in the drip pan.
4. Place on the grill and cook 3-4 hours or until the internal temperature is 165°F (white meat) and 185°F (dark meat). During the cook, cover the turkey with aluminum foil once the skin has the desired color and texture.
5. Remove from the grill, let rest for 15 minutes. Carve and enjoy!
6. Preheat the grill to 350°F using direct heat with a cast iron grate installed.
7. Coat the dutch oven lid with extra virgin olive oil. Place all vegetables into the dutch oven lid. In a bowl, mix melted butter, Worcestershire sauce, pepper and salt. Pour evenly over the top of the vegetables.
8. Roast for 45 minutes, remove from the grill and serve.
9. Preheat the grill to 350°F using direct heat with a cast iron grate installed.
10. Poke holes in the sweet potato, all over. Bake until soft and skin has blistered – about 50 minutes to an hour.
11. Remove from the grill and let rest for 10 minutes. Peel the skin off and discard. Place in a bowl and mash the sweet potatoes. Add salt, and butter and mix thoroughly. Enjoy!

Coconut & Chipotle Braised Chicken Legs

Servings:5
Cooking Time: 27 Minutes

Ingredients:

- 5 Springer Mountain Farms' chicken legs
- Kosher salt and black pepper, to taste
- 1 onion, diced
- 1/4 cup butter
- 3 garlic cloves, smashed with the side of a chef's knife
- 2-3 chipotle peppers from a can of chipotle peppers in adobo, minced
- 1 can coconut milk
- 1 cup basmati rice, cooked
- 1 tbsp cilantro leaves, whole
- 1 lime, cut into wedges

Directions:

1. Preheat the grill to 350°F using direct heat with a cast iron grate installed.
2. Season the chicken generously with salt and pepper, and leave to rest for 30 minutes.
3. Grill the chicken for 2 minutes, or until the meat begins to turn golden brown, flip and cook for another 2 minutes.
4. While the chicken is cooking, heat a cast iron dutch oven or stainless-steel pot on the grid. Add the butter, onion, and garlic. Cook for 2-3 minutes or until the mixture becomes fragrant. Add peppers and coconut milk and allow to simmer.
5. Once the coconut milk begins to simmer, add the chicken legs and cover the dutch oven with the lid. Cook for 20 minutes or until the internal temperature of the chicken passes 165°F and the meat begins to pull away from the bone. Remove the pot from the kamado grill and allow to cool, uncovered. Taste and adjust seasoning.
6. Serve the chicken and sauce over the rice and garnish with cilantro and limes.

Smoked Brined Turkey

Servings:8
Cooking Time: 15 Minutes

Ingredients:

- 1 gallon water
- ½ cup firmly packed brown sugar
- Rind of 1 navel orange
- 3 sprigs rosemary
- 1 cup kosher salt
- 3 yellow onions, quartered
- 1 garlic head
- 2 lemons, quartered
- 1 turkey, appx. 12 lbs
- 10 sprigs thyme
- 10 sprigs sage
- 3 cups chopped potatoes
- ¼ cup olive oil
- Freshly ground black pepper
- Garlic powder

Directions:

1. BRINE: Pour the water into a large bowl. Add the brown sugar, orange rind, rosemary, salt, two-thirds of the quartered lemons and onions and 1 halved garlic head. Mix until the sugar and salt dissolve.
2. Remove the giblets from inside the turkey and reserve for another use. Rinse the turkey well. Place the turkey in a 2 1/2 gallon resealable plastic bag or any container that is large enough to hold the turkey and the liquid. Pour the brine over the turkey, making sure it's completely covered. Refrigerate for 12 hours, turning occasionally.
3. Soak 2 cups of hickory or pecan chips in water for 1 hour.
4. Preheat the grill to 325°F using direct heat with a cast iron grate installed.
5. Remove the turkey from the brine, rinse well to remove the brining liquid and pat dry with paper towels. Discard the brining liquid and solids. Stuff the turkey with the remaining lemon and onion quarters, the remaining halved garlic head, thyme, sage, and 1 cup potatoes. Brush the turkey with olive oil and season with pepper and garlic powder.
6. Place the turkey on the Roasting Rack in a Drip Pan; scatter the remaining potatoes in the pan and place the pan in the kamado grill. Cook for 12 minutes per pound until the turkey has reached a safe minimum internal temperature of 165°F/74°C throughout the product. If the turkey starts to brown too quickly, carefully tent the turkey with aluminum foil. Reserve the drippings from the drip pan to make gravy.
7. Remove the turkey from the kamado grill and let rest for 15 to 20 minutes. Carve and serve immediately.

Southwest Turkey Burgers

Servings:4
Cooking Time: 10 Minutes

Ingredients:

- 4 Nature's Own 100% Whole Wheat Sandwich Rolls
- 1/3 cup salsa
- 1/4 cup chopped green onions
- 1 teaspoon dried oregano leaves
- 1/2 teaspoon ground cumin
- 1/4 teaspoon salt
- 1 small ripe avocado, mashed
- 1 tablespoon reduced-fat sour cream
- 1 tablespoon chopped fresh cilantro
- 1 tablespoon lime juice
- 4 lettuce leaves
- 1 pound ground turkey breast
- 4 tomato slices

Directions:

1. Preheat the grill to 450°F using direct heat with a cast iron grate installed.
2. Combine turkey, salsa, green onions, oregano, cumin and salt in large bowl. Shape into four patties. Place patties on grid and grill 4 to 5 minutes per side or until burgers are cooked through.
3. Meanwhile, combine avocado, sour cream, cilantro and lime juice in medium bowl. Season with salt; set aside. Place lettuce leaf on each roll bottom. Top with burger, tomato slice and avocado mixture.

Hoisin Glazed Wings

Servings: 4
Cooking Time: 30 Minutes

Ingredients:

- 3-4 lbs chicken wings
- 1 cup Chinese Barbecue Sauce
- 1/4 cup Asian Rub

Directions:

1. Liberally dust the wings with the Asian Rub. Set aside.
2. Grilling:
3. Preheat the grill to 400°F using direct heat with a cast iron grate installed.
4. Place the wings on the grid with the dome closed for 20-30 minutes, turning once halfway through cooking.
5. When the juices run clear, place the wings in a large bowl and pour the Chinese Barbecue Sauce Sauce over them. Toss to coat.
6. Replace the wings on the grid and close all of the vents. Allow the wings to finish for 5 minutes.
7. Toss in the sauce once more and serve.

The Best Turkey Burger Ever

Servings: 4
Cooking Time: 12 Minutes

Ingredients:

- 1 1/2 pounds ground turkey (a mixture of white and dark meat is best)
- 1/2 cup fresh breadcrumbs
- 1/4 cup shredded onion
- 1/4 cup shredded Granny Smith apple
- 1/2 tsp salt
- 1/4 tsp pepper
- 1 egg, beaten
- 1 clove garlic, grated
- 1/4 cup mayonnaise
- 2 Tablespoon Besto Pesto
- 1/2 tsp sriracha
- 1 cup arugula
- 4 brioche buns
- 1 Granny Smith apple, thinly sliced

Directions:

1. In a large bowl, combine burger ingredients well. Form into 4 patties and refrigerate while the grill comes to temperature.
2. Grilling:
3. Preheat the grill to 450°F using direct heat with a cast iron grate installed.
4. Place turkey burgers onto the grid and close the dome for 3 minutes.
5. Flip the burgers and close the dome for another 3 minutes.
6. Close all of the vents and allow the burgers to sit for 5 minutes more or until the internal temperature reaches 170°F.
7. Stir together aioli mixture.
8. Remove the burgers and serve on a toasted brioche bun with arugula, thinly sliced apple, and a healthy smear of the aioli.

Chicken Kebobs

Servings:4
Cooking Time: 12 Minutes

Ingredients:

- ½ cup olive oil
- 2 tbsp Citrus & Dill Seasoning
- 2 tsp salt
- ¼ tsp ground black pepper, or to taste
- 1 tsp lemon juice
- 5 boneless, skinless chicken breasts, cut into 1-inch cubes
- ½ cup sour cream
- ½ cup yogurt
- Citrus & Dill Seasoning, to taste
- Squeeze of lemon, optional

Directions:

1. Preheat the grill to 400°F using direct heat with a cast iron grate installed.
2. In a medium bowl, stir together the olive oil, seasoning, salt, pepper and lemon juice; let stand for 5 minutes. Add the chicken to the bowl and stir to coat with the marinade. Cover and refrigerate for 30 minutes. Combine sauce ingredients together and chill in the refrigerator for 15 minutes.
3. Thread chicken onto skewers and discard marinade. Lightly oil the cooking grid. Grill skewers for 8 to 12 minutes or until the chicken is no longer pink in the center and the juices run clear. Serve with the Creamy Citrus & Dill Sauce on the side.

Alma Roja Chicken Wings

Servings:6
Cooking Time: 40 Minutes

Ingredients:

- 3 dozen Springer Mountain Farms Chicken Wings
- 12.5-ounce bottle Valentina Hot Sauce
- 5 tbsp guajillo peppers, deseeded and ground
- 3 tbsp ancho chiles, deseeded and ground
- 3 tbsp pasilla chiles, deseeded and ground
- 2 tbsp sugar
- 1 bunch cilantro
- ¼ lb. butter, softened
- 2 onions
- 1 carrot
- 1 celery rib
- 1 bunch cilantro
- 4 tbsp salt
- 5 qt water

Directions:

1. Preheat the grill to 375°F using direct heat with a cast iron grate installed. Cook for about 30 minutes, turning occasionally, until the internal temperature reached 165°F or higher.
2. After wings are finished, toss the wings in batches with the sauce to coat. Don't make them too saucy or the will burn easily with the sugar.
3. Place wings on the kamado grill without touching each other to get grill marks on both sides. Toss once more in the sauce. Serve immediately with chopped cilantro and lime wedges.
4. For the sauce mix all ingredients together in blender, working in small batches.
5. Cook wings in the poaching liquid for about 10 minutes.

Chipotle Barbecued Turkey Burgers

Servings:8
Cooking Time: 10 Minutes

Ingredients:

- 8 Nature's Own Butter Hamburger Buns
- 1 cup ketchup
- 1/3 cup light brown sugar
- 2 canned chipotle peppers in adobo sauce, minced
- 2 tablespoons cider vinegar
- 3 teaspoon lime juice
- 1/2 teaspoon garlic powder
- 2 medium or 3 small ripe avocados, cut in half and pitted
- 1/8 teaspoon salt, or to taste
- 2 packages (16 ounces each) Butterball Fresh Turkey Burger Patties
- Thinly sliced red onions

Directions:

1. Spray cold grate of kamado grill with cooking spray.Preheat the grill to 350°F using direct heat with a cast iron grate installed.
2. To make barbecue sauce, combine ketchup, brown sugar, peppers, vinegar, 2 teaspoons lime juice and garlic powder in a medium saucepan. Heat until sauce simmers for 3 minutes. Transfer to a bowl to cool.
3. To make guacamole, scoop avocado pulp into a medium bowl. Mash with a fork until mixture is slightly chunky. Stir in 1 teaspoon lime juice and about 1/8 teaspoon salt. Cover tightly with plastic wrap. Set aside.
4. Season turkey patties with salt. Cook 5 to 6 minutes over medium heat. Turn patties and cook 4 minutes.
5. Reserve about half the barbecue sauce. Brush remaining sauce onto patties. Cook until patties are no longer pink in centers and meat thermometer inserted in centers reaches 165°F.
6. Meanwhile, toast insides of sandwich rolls. To assemble burgers, place patties on bun bottoms. Top with reserved sauce if desired. Add onion slices and guacamole.

Chicken Tikka Masala

Servings:4
Cooking Time: 30 Minutes

Ingredients:

- 1 cup plain yogurt
- 2 garlic cloves, minced
- 1 tbsp grated fresh ginger
- 1½ tsp ground cumin
- 1½ tsp ground coriander
- ¼ tsp ground cardamom
- ¼ tsp cayenne pepper
- ¼ tsp ground turmeric
- Salt and pepper
- 2½ lbs. skinless, boneless chicken thighs, fat trimmed
- Salt and pepper
- 2 tbsp plus 1 tsp olive oil
- ¼ cup blanched whole almonds
- 1 large onion, finely chopped
- 2 garlic cloves, minced
- 1 tsp minced fresh ginger
- 1½ tbsp garam masala
- 1 tsp ground cumin
- 1 tsp ground coriander
- ½ tsp cayenne pepper
- One 35-ounce can peeled tomatoes, finely chopped, juices reserved
- Pinch of sugar
- 1 cup heavy cream

Directions:

1. In a bowl combine the yogurt, garlic, ginger, cumin, coriander, cardamom, cayenne and turmeric. Season with salt and pepper. Make slashes in each piece of chicken then add the chicken to the marinade, toss to coat and refrigerate overnight.
2. Preheat the grill to 400°F using direct heat with a cast iron grate installed.
3. Remove the chicken from the marinade and scrape off as much of the marinade as possible. Season the chicken with salt and pepper and cook for 4 minutes per side. Remove from the kamado grill and cut it into 2-inch pieces. Set aside.
4. In a small skillet, heat 1 teaspoon of the oil and add the almonds, cook over medium heat, stirring constantly until golden (about 5 minutes). Transfer the almonds to a plate and let cool completely.
5. In a food processor, pulse the almonds until finely ground.
6. Preheat a dutch oven on the kamado grill. Heat the remaining 2 tablespoons of oil and then add the onion, garlic, and ginger. Cook until the onions are tender and golden, about 8 minutes, stirring occasionally. Add the tomatoes with their juices, sugar and season with salt and pepper. Let reduce until the sauce is slightly thickened, about 20 minutes.
7. Add the garam masala, cumin, coriander, cayenne, and ground almonds. Stir until everything is combined, about 1 minute. Mix in the cream and chicken. Simmer for 10 minutes, stirring frequently. Remove from the kamado grill and serve with naan.

Greg Bates Bbq Chicken

Servings:8
Cooking Time: 30 Minutes

Ingredients:

- Trimmed chicken Breasts
- 2 cups Dr Pepper
- 2 cups ketchup
- ½ cup no-pulp orange juice
- ¼ cup Worcestershire sauce
- ¼ cup molasses
- 1 tsp ground ginger
- 1 tsp hot paprika
- 1 tsp chipotle Chile powder
- 2 tsp garlic powder
- 2 tsp onion powder
- ½ teaspoon crushed red pepper flakes

Directions:

1. Preheat the grill to 450°F using direct heat with a cast iron grate installed.
2. On your grill over medium high heat for 10 to 15 minutes on each side, brushing the Dr Pepper BBQ sauce on the chicken each time you turn it over. Grill until chicken is cooked through and juices run clear.
3. Mix the Dr Pepper, ketchup, orange juice, Worcestershire sauce and molasses in a saucepan. Season with paprika, ginger, garlic powder, red pepper flakes, chipotle powder and onion powder. Bring the sauce to a boil over high heat, proceed to reduce to medium-low heat and simmer for 15 minutes while stirring occasionally.
4. Use right away on your BBQ chicken, or store in your fridge for about a week! Enjoy.

Grilled Chicken Arugula Pesto Wings

Servings:4
Cooking Time: 20 Minutes

Ingredients:

- 2 pounds chicken wings, tips trimmed
- 2 teaspoons Better Than Bouillon Seasoned Vegetable Base
- 1 (4 ounce) package of Baby Arugula
- 1 Tablespoon minced garlic
- 1 Tablespoon freshly squeezed lemon juice
- 1/2 teaspoon cracked black pepper
- 3/4 cup grated Parmesan cheese, divided
- 1/2 cup olive oil

Directions:

1. Add the Seasoned Vegetable Base, arugula, garlic, lemon juice, black pepper and 1/4 cup of the Parmesan cheese to the bowl of a food processor fitted with the steel blade. Pulse for 30 seconds. While the machine is running slowly drizzle in the olive oil until the pesto is combined.
2. Add the pesto to a re-sealable plastic bag, add the wings, toss to coat and refrigerate for 2 hours or up to 8 hours.
3. Preheat the grill to 450°F using direct heat with a cast iron grate installed.
4. Remove the wings from the pesto and place directly onto the kamado grill. Grill the wings for 10 minutes per side.
5. Remove the wings from the kamado grill and sprinkle with the remaining grated Parmesan cheese. Serve immediately.

BEEF

Italian Sausage Sliders

Servings:16
Cooking Time: 6 Minutes

Ingredients:

- 2 pounds Johnsonville All Natural Ground Italian Sausage or Links (remove from casing)
- 1 pound ground beef
- 16 small slider buns or mini sandwich rolls
- Condiments
- Provolone cheese and Marinara sauce
- Fresh mozzarella, fresh basil, and sliced tomatoes
- Giardiniera – marinated chopped vegetables and olives
- Sauteed onions and roasted red peppers
- Sauteed mushrooms and Cheddar cheese

Directions:

1. Preheat the grill to 400°F using direct heat with a cast iron grate installed.
2. In a large bowl, combine sausage and beef. Using your hands, blend the two meats together and form into one large ball. Use a spoon or a small measuring cup to gather up about a 3 ounce ball and press into patties ... with the Mini Burger Basket you can form and cook 12 Mini Burgers at once!
3. Place the Mini Burger Basket or individual sliders directly on the cooking grid. Cook for about 3 minutes then flip and continue cooking for another 3 minutes. The internal temperature should be 160°F.
4. Slice the buns and top the sliders with your favorite condiments.

Cindy's Steak Marsala

Servings:4
Cooking Time: 45 Minutes

Ingredients:

- 4 (4 oz) tenderloin steaks
- 2 tablespoons olive oil
- 1 small onion, finely sliced
- 2 garlic cloves, minced
- 1 tablespoon fresh thyme, minced
- 12 cherry tomatoes, sliced in half
- ½ cup Marsala wine
- ¼ cup low sodium beef broth
- 2 tablespoons dijon mustard
- 2 cups half & half
- 1 teaspoon sea salt
- ¾ teaspoon freshly ground black pepper
- 2 tablespoons basil, chopped
- 1 box penne pasta
- Fresh parmesan cheese for serving

Directions:

1. Preheat the grill to 650°F using direct heat with a cast iron grate installed.
2. In a large sauté pan over medium heat add olive oil and the onions. Cook for about 5 minutes, stirring occasionally, until they are golden brown. Add in cherry tomatoes, garlic and thyme and cook for about 6 minutes. Keeping the heat on medium, stir in the marsala wine, deglazing the pan. Add the beef broth and the dijon mustard and whisk until it is all incorporated. Whisk in half and half then season with salt and pepper and lower the temperature. Cook for about 5 minutes, or until the sauce starts to thicken.
3. In a large pot of boiling water cook the penne pasta (add 2 tablespoons of salt) for about 11 minutes or follow package directions. Drain (except for 1 cup for reserve). If too thick then add in some of the pasta liquid.
4. Add the tenderloins to the center of the cooking grid on the grill. Grill for 3 minutes one side (time it for 3 minutes – DO NOT touch the meat) then flip and shut off the kamado grill and let the tenderloin grill for 3 minutes (or more if you want your steak well done).
5. Add pasta into the sauce pan and coat with the Marsala mixture for 1 minute. Remove from heat, add the steaks and basil and serve immediately with parmesan cheese.

New York Strip Steaks

Servings: 8
Cooking Time: 10 Minutes

Ingredients:

- 4 New York Strip Steaks
- 1/4 cup spice rub of your choice

Directions:

1. Season both sides of all steaks with spice rub and allow to sit for 15 minutes.
2. Grilling:
3. Preheat the grill to 500°F using direct heat with a cast iron grate installed.
4. Place steaks on the grid and close the dome for 3 minutes.
5. Flip the steaks over and cook an additional 2 minutes.
6. Close all of the vents and let the steaks sit for 5 minutes or until the internal temperature reaches 130°F.
7. Allow the steaks to rest for 10 minutes before slicing.

Bacon Cheeseburger Hotdogs

Servings:8
Cooking Time: 16 Minutes

Ingredients:

- 8 good-quality all-beef hot dogs
- 8 Cobblestone Bread Co.™ Spud Dogs
- drizzle of ketchup
- drizzle of mustard
- chopped fresh parsley
- cheeseburger mixture
- white cheddar cheese sauce
- 6 strips of bacon, diced
- 1 pound ground beef
- 1-14 ounce can diced tomatoes, drained
- 2 tablespoons ketchup
- 1 tablespoon yellow mustard
- 1 ½ cups grated sharp cheddar cheese, divided
- salt and black pepper
- 2 tablespoons unsalted butter
- 2 tablespoons all-purpose flour
- 1 ½ cups whole milk
- 1 ½ cup grated white cheddar cheese
- pinch of cayenne pepper
- salt and black pepper

Directions:

1. Preheat the grill to 425°F using direct heat with a cast iron grate installed, and add your hot dogs to the grill. Grill for about 2 minutes on each side or until charred and warm. Remove from heat.
2. Assemble your bacon cheeseburger hot dogs, by placing each hot dog on Cobblestone Bread Co.™ Spud Dog. Top with the cheeseburger mixture and spoon the cheese sauce on top. Drizzle with ketchup and yellow mustard. Sprinkle with fresh parsley and the reserved bacon. Enjoy!
3. In a large, nonstick skillet, add the bacon. Fry over medium-low heat until crispy. Transfer the bacon to a plate that has been lined with a paper towel and pour out most of the bacon grease from the skillet. Place it back on the stove, and increase the heat to medium. Add the beef to the pan and cook until brown and cooked through, about 8 minutes. Decrease the heat to low, and add most of the bacon (reserving about 2 tablespoons for garnish) diced tomatoes, ketchup, yellow mustard, cheddar cheese, and salt and black pepper. Stir until the cheese has melted. Cover and keep warm.
4. In a small saucepan, melt the butter for the white cheddar cheese sauce over medium heat. Whisk in the flour and cook for about 1 minute or until golden. Continuing to whisk, add the milk. Cook for about 3-4 minutes or until just slightly thickened. Remove from heat and stir in the white cheddar cheese until melted. Season with a pinch of cayenne pepper and salt and black pepper to taste. Cover and keep warm until you are ready to serve.

Grilled Entrecôte Of Beef

Servings:4
Cooking Time: 20 Minutes

Ingredients:

- Guacamole
- Spice Rub and Entrecote
- Cheesy Tortillas
- 2 Ripe Avocados
- 1 Red Onion, Finely Chopped
- 2 Tomatoes, Inside Removed, then Cubed
- 1/2 Cup (120 ml) Cilantro, Roughly Chopped
- 1 Lemon, Zest and Juice
- 4 Ribeye Steaks
- 2 tbsp (30g) Coarse Salt
- 1 1/2 tbsp (20g) Surgar
- 2 tbsp (15g) Coriander Powder
- 2 tbsp (15g) Paprika
- 2 tbsp (5g) Garlic Flakes
- 1/2 tbsp (5g) Peppercorns
- 2 tbsp (5g) Onion Powder
- 2 tbsp (5g) Fresh Thyme
- 4 Tortillas
- 1/2 Cup (60g) Cheddar Cheese, Grated
- 1/3 Cup (80 ml) Parsley, Roughly Chopped
- Cayenne Pepper
- Lemon Zest

Directions:

1. Preheat the grill to 750°F using direct heat with a cast iron grate installed. Place the steaks on the grill and cook to the desired temperature. While the meat is resting before carving, lower the temperature to 400°F and place the tortillas on the grill, allowing the cheese to melt and the tortillas to get a crust. Cut the tortillas into quarters and serve with the guacamole.
2. Mesh the avocado to desired texture with a fork. Add the rest of the ingredients and mix well. Season to taste.
3. Place all rub ingredients in a mortar and pestle or spice grinder, and grind to just before it becomes fine. Rub generously over the steaks and refrigerate for an hour.
4. Mix all the ingredients and spread evenly over tortillas. Cover with the remaining tortillas and lightly press down. Be careful before braaing as the cheese may fall out.

Pastrami Beef Short Ribs

Servings:8
Cooking Time: 120 Minutes

Ingredients:

- 1 Whole Snake River Farms Beef Plate Short Rib
- Corning Brine
- Pastrami Rub
- 1 gallon water
- 1½ cups Kosher salt
- ¾ cups granulated sugar
- ¾ cups brown sugar
- 1 Tbsp + 2 tsp Tinted Cure Mix #1 (Pink Salt)
- 4 bay leaves, crushed
- 1 Tbsp juniper berries, crushed
- 10 cloves, whole
- 1 Tbsp black peppercorns, crushed
- 1 Tbsp coriander seeds, crushed
- 1 Tbsp mustard seeds
- 5 garlic cloves, crushed
- ¼ cup honey
- 1 cup black peppercorns, coarsely ground
- ½ cup coriander seeds, coarsely ground
- ½ cup onion powder
- ½ cup granulated garlic powder
- ¼ cup juniper berries, ground

Directions:

1. Combine all of the brine ingredients in a large pot and bring to a simmer. Simmer for 15 minutes, then cool and store overnight in the refrigerator. Place the whole short rib in a 2 gallon zipper bag. Then pour the cold brine in the bag. The bag should hold the full gallon of brine. Let the rib brine for a minimum of 48 hours. Flip the bag over each day.
2. Grind the peppercorns and coriander seeds in a mortar and pestle or a coffee grinder for the best results. Start with a full cup of each before you grind them. After grinding, combine the peppercorns and coriander seeds with the onion powder, garlic powder and the ground Juniper berries.
3. Remove the short rib from the brine. Pat dry with a paper towel. Liberally coat the rib with the pastrami rub. Do not be afraid to go heavy with this rub!
4. Preheat the grill to 275°F using direct heat with a cast iron grate installed.
5. Place the short ribs meat side up in the smoker. Smoke the ribs for two hours at 275°F. Next, reduce the temperature to 250°F. Smoke until the rib reaches an internal temperature of 185°F.
6. At this stage, wrap ribs in butcher's paper, or place in a large paper grocery bag. Once wrapped, place back in the smoker until the ribs reach an internal temperature of 203°F. Remove from the smoker and allow the rib to rest in the paper for 20-25 minutes before serving.

Cast Iron Seared T-bone Steak

Servings:4
Cooking Time: 15 Minutes

Ingredients:

- 1 large bone-in T-bone steak, at least 2 in (5 cm) thick
- Kosher salt and freshly ground black pepper
- 1⁄4 cup (60ml) grapeseed or other high smoke-point oil
- 3 tbsp (45g) unsalted butter
- 6 sprigs thyme or rosemary
- 1 large shallot, finely sliced

Directions:

1. Carefully pat the steak dry with a paper towel. Season liberally on all sides, including the edges, with salt and pepper. Let the steak rest at room temperature for 45 minutes.
2. Preheat the grill to 550°F using direct heat with a cast iron grate installed.
3. Add a Cast Iron Skillet to the cooking grid; heat the oil until it shimmers in the skillet. Carefully add the steak and cook, flipping once, until a golden-brown crust starts to develop, about 3 minutes total.
4. Add the butter, herbs and shallot to the skillet and continue to cook, flipping the steak occasionally and basting any light spots with butter. Continue searing and basting until an instant-read thermometer inserted into thickest part of the tenderloin side registers 120–125°F for medium-rare, 6 to 10 minutes total.
5. Transfer the steak to a large platter and pour the juices on top. Let rest 5 to 10 minutes. Carve, serve, enjoy!

Sloppy Joes

Servings: 4
Cooking Time: 40 Minutes

Ingredients:

- 1 lb ground beef
- 1/4 cup onion, finely chopped
- 1/4 cup bell pepper, finely chopped
- 1 clove garlic, finely chopped
- 1/2 cup tomato sauce
- 1/4 cup ketchup
- 2 Tablespoons brown sugar
- 1 Tablespoon brown mustard
- Salt & Pepper

Directions:

1. Preheat the grill to 400°F using direct heat with a cast iron grate installed with the dutch oven on the grid.
2. Place all ingredients in the dutch oven and stir.
3. Cover the dutch oven and lower the dome for 30-40 minutes or until the beef is cooked through.
4. Serve on hamburger buns.

Bacon-wrapped Steakhouse Filet

Servings:2
Cooking Time: 12 Minutes

Ingredients:

- 2 bacon slices
- 2-2½ inch thick filet steaks
- Classic Steakhouse Seasoning
- Extra virgin olive oil
- Skewers

Directions:

1. Preheat the grill to 550°F using direct heat with a cast iron grate installed.
2. On a perforated cooking grid, cook the bacon just until it has firmed up a little bit. Set aside.
3. Coat the steaks with olive oil and season with Classic Steakhouse Seasoning on all sides. Wrap the partially-cooked bacon around the edges of the steak; secure with a skewer.
4. Grill the steaks for 5-6 minutes on each side, or until the internal temperature is 125°F(or to slightly below your desired temperature). Remove from grill and let rest covered for 10 minutes.
5. Slice and serve!

Steakhouse Meatballs With French Fries And Tzatziki Sauce

Servings:4
Cooking Time: 30 Minutes

Ingredients:

- 1 lb. ground beef, 92% lean 8% fat
- 1 tbsp Steakhouse Seasoning
- 2 tbsp fresh parsley, chopped
- ⅓ cup grated Parmesan cheese
- Olive oil
- 1½ cup whole fat plain Greek yogurt
- ¾ cup cucumber, grated
- 2 tbsp fresh dill, chopped
- 2 cloves garlic, finely minced
- 1 tbsp lemon juice
- ½ tsp kosher salt
- 2 tbsp olive oil
- 2 russet potatoes, skin on, cut into lengthwise strips
- 1 qt water
- 2 tbsp Sweet & Smoky Seasoning
- Salt to taste
- 2 tbsp olive oil

Directions:

1. Preheat the grill to 400°F using direct heat with a cast iron grate installed. Place the half-moon cast iron griddle with the flat side up on top of the grid.
2. For the meatballs, mix the ground beef, Steakhouse Seasoning, and Parmesan cheese until uniform. Roll into inch sized balls. Place meatballs on the plancha, and cook until the internal temperature is 140°F. Remove from the kamado grill and let rest.
3. To plate, put a dollop of tzatziki sauce on the plate, top with meatballs, add fries to the side, and garnish with the parsley. Enjoy!
4. For the tzatziki sauce, mix all the ingredients together until uniform and refrigerate until needed.
5. Soak potatoes in water for 30 minutes, and then pat to dry. Let them air dry for 5 to 10 minutes. Coat them in olive oil, a pinch or two of salt and the Sweet & Smoky Seasoning. Place them into the roasting pan, making sure the potatoes are all flat on the pan. Bake for 30 minutes or until the potatoes are golden brown.

Italian Spaghetti Sauce And Meatballs

Servings:12
Cooking Time: 120 Minutes

Ingredients:

- 1 lb. lean ground beef
- 1 cup Italian-style breadcrumbs
- 3 tbsp grated Parmesan cheese
- 3 tablespoons fresh parsley, chopped
- 1 clove garlic, minced
- ¼ tsp freshly ground black pepper
- 1 egg, beaten
- 1 medium onion, chopped
- 4 cloves garlic, divided, minced
- 1/4 cup olive oil
- 2 (28 ounce) cans whole peeled tomatoes
- 1 tsp white sugar
- 1½ tsp salt
- 1 bay leaf
- 1 (6 ounce) can tomato paste
- ¾ tsp dried basil
- ½ tsp freshly ground black pepper

Directions:

1. In a large bowl, combine the ground beef, breadcrumbs, cheese, parsley, garlic, black pepper and beaten egg. Mix well and form into 12 balls. Cover and store in the refrigerator until needed.
2. Preheat the grill to 350°F using direct heat with a cast iron grate installed. Add a cast iron skillet to preheat, then sauté the garlic and onion in olive oil until the onion is translucent. Stir in the tomatoes, sugar, salt and bay leaf, breaking up any large chunks of tomato. Simmer 90 minutes, stirring occasionally. Stir in the tomato paste, basil and pepper. Add the meatballs and simmer 30 minutes more. Serve alone or over pasta.

Jim Beam Hamburgers

Servings:2
Cooking Time: 12 Minutes

Ingredients:

- 1 pound ground beef
- 1 (1 oz) package onion soup mix
- 2 tablespoons Worcestershire sauce
- 2 tablespoons Jim Beam bourbon
- Dash hot pepper sauce (recommended: Tabasco)
- Hamburger buns, for serving

Directions:

1. Preheat the grill to 375°F using direct heat with a cast iron grate installed. Using your hands, combine all ingredients in a medium bowl, mixing just to combine. Divide meat into 4 portions and form each into patty using your hands. Grill for 4 to 6 minutes on both sides for medium-rare to medium doneness. If desired, place buns, cut side down on the grill, until toasted, about 1 to 2 minutes. Serve burgers on buns.

Aged Prime Rib

Servings: 8
Cooking Time: 120 Minutes

Ingredients:

- 2 tsp garlic salt
- 2 tsp onion salt
- 2 tsp kosher salt
- 1 tsp freshly ground black pepper
- 2 tsp dried rosemary
- 4lb (1.8kg) bone-in prime rib roast, aged for at least 28 days
- 3 garlic cloves, slivered
- 1/2 to 1 cup beef stock, as needed
- for the marrow butter
- 2 beef marrow bones, cut in half lengthwise at the butcher
- 1/2lb (225g) butter, softened
- 3/4 tsp chopped fresh flat-leaf parsley
- kosher salt and freshly ground black pepper
- to smoke
- hickory or oak wood chunks

Directions:

1. In a medium bowl, combine garlic salt, onion salt, kosher salt, pepper, and rosemary. Place roast in a baking dish and use a sharp knife to cut tiny slits every 2 inches (5cm), and insert the garlic slivers in the slits. Rub the roast with the spice mixture, cover with plastic wrap, and refrigerate for 24 hours.
2. Preheat the grill to 225°F (107°C). Once hot, add the wood chunks, install the heat deflector with a drip pan placed on top, and install a standard grate. Place roast and marrow bones on the grate, close the lid, and smoke until the internal temperature of the meat reaches 125°F (52°C), about 2 hours. Transfer roast to a large platter, cover with aluminum foil, and set aside to rest.
3. Remove the bones from the grill, and use a spoon to scrape the marrow from the bones into a medium bowl. To make the marrow butter, add butter and parsley to the marrow, and mix until well combined. Season with salt and pepper to taste. Set aside.
4. Remove the drip pan from the grill and pour the drippings into a medium all-metal saucepan. Place the saucepan on the heat deflector, close the lid, and heat for10 minutes, adding beef stock as needed. Season with salt and pepper to taste.
5. Place roast on a cutting board and slice. Serve immediately with the marrow butter and warm jus for dipping.

Asian Beef & Mushroom Tacos

Servings: 4
Cooking Time: 25 Minutes

Ingredients:

- 1⁄2 head of green cabbage
- 1lb (450g) flank or round steak, cut into very thin strips
- kosher salt and freshly ground black pepper
- 3 tbsp vegetable oil, divided
- 1lb (450g) white mushrooms, sliced
- 4oz (110g) shredded carrots, fresh or pickled
- 1⁄3 cup hoisin sauce, plus more for serving
- 8 x 6-in (15.25-cm) flour tortillas
- 1⁄4 cup chopped fresh cilantro

Directions:

1. Preheat the grill to 425°F (218°C) using direct heat with a standard grate installed and a cast iron skillet on the grate. Place cabbage on the grate (not in the skillet) cut side down, close the lid, and grill until beginning to soften and char, about 7 to 10 minutes. Remove cabbage from the grill and slice finely. Set aside.
2. Season beef well with salt and pepper. Add 2 tbsp oil to the hot skillet and heat until shimmering. Add beef and cook until the meat has browned on both sides, about 5 to 6 minutes, turning once. Transfer to a platter and set aside. Return the skillet to the grill.
3. Add the remaining 1 tbsp oil to the skillet and heat until shimmering. Add mushrooms and cook until they're tender and all the liquid has evaporated, about 5 minutes. Add carrots and sliced cabbage to the skillet and cook until beginning to soften, about 2 minutes, stirring once or twice. Add the hoisin sauce and beef, stir to coat, and cook for 1 minute more.
4. Remove the taco mixture from the grill. To serve, scoop an equal portion of the mixture into each tortilla and top with cilantro and more hoisin sauce (if desired).

PORK

Smoked Andouille & Crawfish Gumbo

Servings: 12
Cooking Time: 180 Minutes

Ingredients:

- 1 green bell pepper, left whole
- 1 large yellow onion, halved
- 3 stalks of celery, left whole
- 11/2 cups vegetable oil
- 1/2 cups all-purpose flour
- 1/2lb (225g) andouille sausage
- 1lb (450g) smoked sausage
- 8 cups chicken stock
- 1lb (450g) crawfish meat
- 11/2 tsp kosher salt
- 1/2 tsp ground cayenne pepper (optional)
- 2 tbsp chopped fresh flat-leaf parsley
- 2 tbsp sliced scallions
- 6 cups cooked white rice, to serve (optional)

Directions:

1. Preheat the grill to 325°F (163°C) using direct heat with a cast iron grate installed and a dutch oven on the grate. Place pepper, onion, and celery on the grate around the dutch oven, close the grill lid, and grill until beginning to soften and char, about 6 to 8 minutes. Transfer the vegetables to a cutting board. Seed and dice the pepper, and dice the celery and onion. Set aside.
2. In the hot dutch oven, heat oil until shimmering. Add flour and stir. Close the grill lid and cook for 20 to 25 minutes, stirring every 5 minutes. While the roux cooks, place the sausages on the grate next to the dutch oven, close the grill lid, and grill until slightly charred, about 10 minutes. Remove the sausages from the grill, finely dice andouille and slice smoked sausage into bite-sized pieces.
3. Once the roux looks dark brown in color, add sausages, peppers, onions, and celery to the dutch oven, and stir to coat. Close the grill lid and cook until the vegetables are soft, about 8 to 10 minutes.
4. Add stock to the dutch oven, and stir until the roux and stock are well combined. Leaving the dutch oven uncovered, close the grill lid and reduce the heat by closing the top and bottom vents most of the way. Cook for 90 minutes, stirring occasionally. Add crawfish to the dutch oven, close the grill lid, and cook for 15 minutes more.
5. Remove the dutch oven from the grill and let sit for 5 minutes before skimming any fat that has risen to the surface. Stir in salt and cayenne (if using). Taste and adjust the seasonings as needed. Stir in parsley and scallions, and serve immediately with white rice (if using).

Double Smoked Maple Bourbon Glazed Ham

Servings:4
Cooking Time: 180 Minutes

Ingredients:

- 1 bone-in half spiral ham
- 3 cups apple juice
- 1 yellow onion, chopped
- 2 tbsp yellow mustard
- BBQ rub
- 1/2 cup pineapple juice
- 1/2 cup maple syrup
- 1 cup bourbon
- 1/4 tsp Dijon mustard
- 1 tsp cinnamon
- 1 cup brown sugar

Directions:

1. Preheat the grill to 275°F using direct heat with a cast iron grate installed.
2. Cover the ham in yellow mustard and add the BBQ rub. Put the apple juice and onion in a roasting pan then place the ham in a roasting rack in the roasting pan. Cook uncovered for 2 hours. Cover with foil and cook another hour. Uncover the ham, glaze, and cook for 30 minutes until the ham reaches an internal temperature of 140°.
3. Remove the ham from the kamado grill and let rest for 10 minutes. Slice and serve.
4. Add glaze ingredients to pan, bring to a boil, and reduce. Cook for 30 minutes or to your desired thickness.

Mediterranean Stuffed Chicken

Servings: 4
Cooking Time: 30 Minutes

Ingredients:

- 4 boneless, skinless chicken breasts, about 11⁄2lb (680g) in total
- 3 tbsp extra virgin olive oil
- 2 tbsp kosher salt, plus more as needed
- 2 tbsp ground black pepper, plus more as needed
- 1 tbsp dried marjoram
- for the brine
- 1⁄4 cup kosher salt
- 1⁄4 cup packed light brown sugar
- 2 tbsp pickling spice
- 3 cups hot water
- for the filling
- 8 sun-dried tomatoes in olive oil, drained and minced
- 4 basil leaves, stacked, rolled, and cut crosswise into thin strips
- 4oz (110g) goat cheese, crumbled
- kosher salt and freshly ground black pepper
- to smoke
- apricot, pecan, or wine barrel wood chunks

Directions:

1. To make the brine, in a medium bowl, whisk together salt, brown sugar, pickling spice, and hot water until salt and sugar have dissolved. Add ice cubes a few at a time until the liquid is no longer hot. Place chicken in a large resealable plastic bag and add brine to cover. (Any extra brine can be refrigerated and saved for a later use.) Refrigerate for 30 minutes.
2. To make the filling, in a medium bowl, combine tomatoes, basil, and cheese, and season with salt and pepper to taste.
3. Remove chicken from the brine, pat dry with paper towels, and cut a slit in the side of each chicken breast to create a pocket. Fill the cavities with equal amounts of filling and close up the pockets with toothpicks soaked in water. Lightly coat the breasts with olive oil, and sprinkle with salt, pepper, and marjoram.
4. Preheat the grill to 325°F (163°C). Once hot, add the wood chunks and install the heat deflector and a standard grate. Place chicken on the grate, close the lid, and smoke until chicken reaches an internal temperature of 165°F (74°C), about 20 to 30 minutes.
5. Remove chicken from the grill and serve immediately.

Homemade Bacon

Servings: 10
Cooking Time: 210 Minutes

Ingredients:

- 5 pounds pork belly, skin on
- 1/4 cup Kosher salt
- 1/4 cup dark brown sugar, packed
- 1/4 cup honey
- 2 Tablespoons sweet paprika
- 2 Tablespoons chili powder
- 1 Tablespoon cracked black pepper
- 2 tsp pink curing salt
- 2 cups wood chips, soaked in water for 30 minutes

Directions:

1. Rinse the pork and pat it dry.
2. Mix the cure together and liberally spread it on the pork belly.
3. Place the pork in a large zip top bag, close it and refrigerate it for 7-10 days, flipping every day until the pork feels firm. (7 days for a 1 1/2 inch thick pork belly)
4. Remove the pork from the bag and rinse and dry it thoroughly.
5. Place the pork on a rack over a pan back in the fridge, uncovered, for 48 hours to allow the skin to dry out.
6. Grilling:
7. Preheat the grill to 200°F using direct heat with a cast iron grate installed, putting the drained wood chips on top of the charcoal and putting the plate setter and grid in place.
8. Place the pork belly on the grid and close the dome. Cook for 3 - 3 1/2 hours or until the internal temperature of the pork reaches 150°F.
9. Allow the bacon to cool then remove the rind.
10. Store the bacon wrapped in plastic in the fridge for up to 1 week or in the freezer for up to 2 months.

Baby Back Ribs With Guava Barbecue Sauce

Servings:6

Cooking Time: 250 Minutes

Ingredients:

- 3 tbsp sugar
- 2 tbsp coarse salt (kosher or sea)
- 2 tbsp freshly ground black pepper
- 1 tbsp Chinese dry mustard
- 2 tsp Chinese five-spice powder
- 1 cup Chinese rice wine, sake, or rice vinegar
- 2 racks baby back ribs (4 to 5 pounds total), membranes removed
- 8 ounces guava paste, cut into ½ inch pieces
- ½ cup rice or cider vinegar
- 1/3 cup dark rum
- ¼ cup ketchup or tomato paste
- 3 tbsp fresh lime juice
- 1½ tbsp soy sauce
- 1½ tbsp Worcestershire sauce
- 1 tbsp minced fresh ginger
- 1 tbsp minced scallion white
- ½ tsp ground cinnamon
- ½ tsp ground nutmeg
- ½ tsp ground allspice
- 3 tbsp brown sugar
- Coarse salt (kosher or sea) and fresh ground black pepper to taste

Directions:

1. Preheat the grill to 275°F using direct heat with a cast iron grate installed.
2. Prepare the rub with sugar, salt, pepper, mustard and five spice powder in a bowl and mix. Sprinkle the ribs on both sides with rub, rubbing it into the meat.
3. Arrange the ribs, bone side down. After cooking for 1 hour spray the ribs with rice wine. Cook another 3 to 4 hours and spray the ribs once or twice. When ribs are cooked, the meat will have shrunk back from the ends of the bones by about 1/2-inch.
4. In the last 30 minutes, brush the ribs on both sides with some of the guava barbecue sauce. Grill until the ribs are browned and bubbling, 2 minutes per side.
5. Transfer the ribs to a large platter or cutting board, and cut the racks in half, widthwise (or into individual ribs). Serve at once with the remaining guava sauce on the side.
6. For the guava barbecue sauce, place the guava paste, vinegar, rum, ketchup or tomato paste, lime juice, soy sauce, Worcestershire sauce, ginger, scallion whites, cinnamon, nutmeg, allspice, and salt and pepper in a heavy saucepan. Add 1/4 cup water. Gently simmer the sauce over medium heat until thick and richly flavored, 10 minutes, whisking to break up the pieces of guava paste. The sauce should be thick but pourable—add water as needed. Correct the seasoning, adding salt and pepper to taste.

Smoked Ham On Grill

Servings:10
Cooking Time: 60 Minutes

Ingredients:

- 7-12 lb. ham, not spiral sliced
- 3 cups apple juice - water or other juice can be used
- 2 cups of apples, oranges or other fruits, cut into small pieces
- 1 cup brown sugar
- 1 tsp black pepper
- ¼ cup of bourbon
- ¼ cup of syrup
- 2 tbsp of brown mustard

Directions:

1. Preheat the grill to 275°F using direct heat with a cast iron grate installed. We recommend the apple smoking chips.
2. Fill a drip pan with the juice and fruit and place on the platesetter.
3. Score the fat portion of the ham in a checkerboard pattern, making cuts approximately 1 inch apart, and 1 inch deep.
4. Cook for approximately 1 hour for 2 lbs. of weight. During the last hour of cooking, brush ham with the glaze. Remove when the ham has reached the internal temperature of 155- 160°F.
5. Let the ham rest before serving
6. For the glaze mix all the ingredients together and let sit for 2-3 hours.

Dr. Bbq's Pork Chops

Servings:4
Cooking Time: 13 Minutes

Ingredients:

- 4 boneless pork chops, about ½ inch thick
- 4 medium yellow onions, halved and sliced thin
- 2 cloves garlic, crushed
- Vegetable oil
- BBQ rub
- 4 hamburger buns

Directions:

1. Preheat the grill to 400°F using direct heat with a cast iron grate installed.
2. Add the half cast iron griddle to one side to preheat. Season the chops with the barbecue rub. Add 1 to 2 tablespoons oil to the hot griddle and then add the onions. Season the onions with barbecue rub and sprinkle the garlic powder the top.
3. Cook for about 5 minutes tossing the onions occasionally. Add the pork chops and cook 3 to 4 minutes until golden broiwn. Flip and continue tossing the onions occasionally. Cook another 3 to 4 minutes until the chops are golden brown and have reached an internal temp of 150°F.
4. Remove the chops and onions from the grill. Place a chop on each bun and top with ¼ of the onions.

Bourbon Glazed Pork Tenderloin

Servings:4
Cooking Time: 13 Minutes

Ingredients:

- 1 teaspoon smoked paprika
- 1/4 teaspoon cinnamon
- 1 teaspoon salt
- 2 teaspoons olive oil
- 1/2 cup peach preserves
- 2 tablespoon bourbon
- 2 (1-pound) pork tenderloins, trimmed and silver skin removed
- 5 peaches, unpeeled and cut into quarters

Directions:

1. In a small bowl, combine paprika, cinnamon and salt. Rub tenderloins with olive oil and sprinkle with spice rub.
2. Preheat the grill to 400°F using direct heat with a cast iron grate installed. Grill pork, turning as needed, until lightly charred and meat thermometer inserted in thickest part registers 135°F, about 9 minutes. During the last few minutes of grilling, brush pork with peach glaze to finish.
3. While pork is grilling, place peach quarters on kamado grill for about 2 minutes per side, until lightly charred. Allow pork to rest 10 minutes before slicing. Serve with grilled peaches.

Dutch Oven Pork Roast

Servings: 6
Cooking Time: 75 Minutes

Ingredients:

- 1 3-4 lb boneless pork loin roast
- 2 lbs small potatoes (we like reds or Yukon golds)
- 1 lb parsnips, peeled and cut into 1 inch chunks
- 1 Tablespoon fresh thyme
- Salt and Pepper
- 1/4 cup brown mustard
- 2 Tablespoons Worcestershire sauce
- 2 Tablespoons olive oil

Directions:

1. In a cold dutch oven, toss vegetables with olive oil and a sprinkling of salt and pepper.
2. In a small bowl, combine mustard, Worcestershire, and thyme. Paint all over the loin roast.
3. Place the roast on top of the vegetables.
4. Grilling:
5. Preheat the grill to 425°F using direct heat with a cast iron grate installed.
6. Cover the dutch oven and place on the waiting grill.
7. Lower the dome for 1 hour to 1 hour and 15 minutes or until the internal temperature of the roast reaches 155°F
8. Remove the dutch oven from the grill, remove the pork and set aside to rest for 20 minutes before carving. Recover the dutch oven to keep the vegetables warm in the meantime.
9. Serve warm.

Smoked Porchetta On The Grill

Servings:12

Cooking Time: 370 Minutes

Ingredients:

- 1 pork belly
- 1 cup kosher salt
- 4 star anis, ground
- 10 black peppercorns, ground
- 5 allspice, ground
- 10 white peppercorns, ground
- 10 garlic cloves, smashed
- 3 sprigs thyme, chopped
- ½ cup granulated sugar
- 3 bunches broccoli raab
- 7 garlic cloves, shaved thin
- 1 tbsp butter
- 3 tsp red pepper flakes
- 1 tbsp lemon juice
- Salt and pepper to taste

Directions:

1. Twenty-four hours before your cook, mix all the aromatics together and rub into the pork belly on both sides. Cure the pork belly in a cooler.
2. Preheat the grill to 250°F using direct heat with a cast iron grate installed.
3. Rinse off the cure, then tie the pork belly into a roll with butcher twine. Place the rolled and tied pork belly in the grill. Smoke the belly until tender, around 4-6 hours or until an internal temperature reaches 165°F. Remove from the grill, untie and let rest for 10 minutes.
4. While the pork belly is resting, set up the kamado grill for direct cooking without the platesetter at 400°F.
5. Place the garlic and butter in a cast iron skillet. Cook garlic until it starts to brown then add the broccoli and the remaining ingredients. Cook the broccoli until it starts to wilt, roughly 5 minutes. Tip: add a touch of water if needed to help keep the pan from getting too hot. Remove from kamado grill and serve.
6. Slice the belly to desired thickness and serve with the braised broccoli raab.

Plts - Pork, Lettuce And Tomato Sandwiches

Servings: 6
Cooking Time: 7 Minutes

Ingredients:

- 6 pork loin chops, cut 1/2 inch thick
- 1/2 tsp garlic powder
- 1/2 tsp onion powder
- 1/2 tsp poultry seasoning
- 1/2 tsp salt
- 1/4 tsp pepper
- 1 cup shredded lettuce
- 1/2 cup mayonnaise
- 2 Tablespoons Besto Pesto
- 12 slices tomato
- 6 sesame seed buns

Directions:

1. Place each pork chop between two pieces of plastic wrap and pound flat.
2. Combine seasonings and sprinkle both sides of each pork chop liberally.
3. Grilling:
4. Preheat the grill to 400°F using direct heat with a cast iron grate installed.
5. Place the chops on the grid and close the dome for 2 minutes.
6. Flip the chops and replace the dome for 3-5 minutes or until the pork is just cooked through.
7. Remove the chops and set aside.
8. Combine mayonnaise and pesto and spread the buns liberally with the mixture.
9. Top each bun with a pork chop, lettuce, and tomato.

Pork Chops

Servings:2
Cooking Time: 70 Minutes

Ingredients:

- 4 10-oz (283 g) bone-in pork chops (about ½ in (13 mm) thick)
- 4 cups (32 oz) Sweet Tea Brine (recipe follows)
- 2 tbsp (30 ml) blended olive oil
- 1 tsp (5 ml) kosher salt
- 1 tsp (5 ml) coarsely ground black pepper
- ½ cup (4 oz) bourbon
- ¼ cup (2 oz) unsalted butter
- Apple Butter and Spiced Pumpkin Seeds (recipe follows)
- ½ cup (4 oz) unsalted butter, melted
- 8 red apples, cored
- ¼ cup (60 ml) packed light brown sugar
- 1 tsp (5 ml) ground cinnamon
- ½ tsp (3 ml) ground cloves
- ½ tsp (3 ml) ground allspice
- ½ tsp (3 ml) kosher salt
- Pinch of freshly ground black pepper
- 2 tbsp (30 ml) blended olive oil
- 1 cup (240 ml) pumpkin seeds
- ½ tsp (3 ml) gray sea salt
- ½ tsp (3 ml) curry powder
- ¼ tsp (1.5 ml) freshly ground black pepper
- 8 cups (64 oz water)
- 8 regular-size orange pekoe black tea bags
- 1 cup (240 ml) granulated sugar
- 1 cup (240 ml) kosher salt
- 1 tbsp (15 ml) black peppercorns
- ¼ tsp (1.5 ml) red pepper flakes
- 4 garlic cloves
- 4 star anise pods
- 4 bay leaves
- 2 large thyme sprigs
- 2 medium-size oranges, cut into quarters
- 1 large lemon, cut into quarters

Directions:

1. Combine the pork and Sweet Tea Brine in a large baking dish. Cover and refrigerate 8 hours or overnight.
2. Remove the pork chops from the brine; discard brine. Let the pork chops come to room temperature, about 30 minutes. Rub the pork chops with the oil, and sprinkle evenly with the salt and pepper.
3. Bring the bourbon to a simmer in a saucepan over medium heat. Cook until reduced by half, about 8 minutes. Remove from the heat and whisk in the butter. Set aside.
4. Preheat the grill to 450°F using direct heat with a cast iron grate installed.
5. Grill the pork chops until golden brown and slightly crispy on the bottom, about 6 minutes, basting occasionally with the bourbon butter. Turn the pork chops and cook until the meat begins to draw close to the bone, about 4 minutes.
6. Transfer to a wire rack; let stand 15 minutes, basting occasionally with any remaining bourbon butter. Serve with Apple Butter, Spiced Pumpkin Seeds and collard greens as a side.
7. Set the kamado grill for indirect cooking with the platesetter at 350F. Combine the melted butter and apples in a baking dish, turning to coat the apples in the butter. Bake until the apples are very tender and the skins pop, 50 minutes to 1 hour. Sprinkle the apples with the brown sugar, cinnamon, cloves, allspice, kosher salt and pepper. Return to the kamado grill until the sugar melts, about 5 minutes. Remove from the grill, and let stand 15 minutes. Transfer the apple mixture to a blender and process until smooth. Let stand 30 minutes at room temperature or refrigerate overnight.
8. Set the kamado grill for indirect cooking with the platesetter at 350F. Heat the oil in a cast iron skillet in the grill; add the pumpkin seeds and cook, stirring occasionally, until golden brown, about 2 minutes. Remove from the grill. Stir in the sea salt, curry powder, and pepper. Drain on a plate lined with paper towels.
9. Bring the water just to boiling in a large saucepan. Remove from the heat and add the tea bags. Let stand 5 minutes; remove and discard the tea bags. Add the remaining ingredients, squeezing the citrus juice into the pan as you add them. Return to medium-high and bring to a simmer. Remove from heat and let stand 1 hour. Remove the solids and store in an airtight container in the refrigerator up to 5 days.

Breakfast Fatty

Servings:8
Cooking Time: 90 Minutes

Ingredients:

- 1 package of bacon
- 1 package of breakfast sausage
- 5 large eggs
- 1 cup of shredded cheese (3 cheese blend works well)
- ½ white onion, chopped
- ½ green bell pepper, chopped
- Meat Church Honey Hog BBQ Rub
- Salt & pepper

Directions:

1. Preheat the grill to 275°F using direct heat with a cast iron grate installed.
2. Start by lightly sautéing the onions and bell peppers on the Half Moon Plancha Griddle. Scramble the eggs and add the onion and bell pepper mixture. Salt and pepper to taste and set aside.
3. Next make a 6×6 bacon weave. Lay 6 pieces of bacon side by side (touching) on parchment paper, which will help to prevent sticking. Then weave the remaining 6 pieces of bacon across those 6. Make sure your bacon weave is tight.
4. Next layer the breakfast sausage evenly across your bacon weave. Make sure the sausage extends to the edges of the bacon weave.
5. Add the scrambled egg mixture evenly across the sausage. Then spread the shredded cheese evenly across the top of the eggs. Top with a sprinkling of Honey Hog BBQ rub.
6. Carefully roll the bacon weave up tightly to form what looks like a burrito. Tuck the ends of the bacon into the side of the breakfast fatty to secure all the contents.
7. Cover all sides with a nice coat of Honey Hog BBQ rub.
8. Place the breakfast fatty on the grid and cook until the internal temperature reaches at least 160°F. That will ensure the ground sausage is fully cooked. This will take about 1 ½ hours.
9. Remove the breakfast fatty from the cooker and let rest for at least 10 minutes. Slice 1" thick slices. This is great by itself, on a biscuit or as Matt does in Texas, on a fresh flour tortilla!

Maple Bourbon Pork Chops

Servings:4
Cooking Time: 6 Minutes

Ingredients:

- 4 boneless center cut pork chops
- ¾ cup bourbon
- 3 tablespoons brown sugar
- 1 garlic clove, minced
- 1 teaspoon apple cider vinegar
- 1 tablespoons worcestershire sauce
- 2 tablespoons pure maple syrup
- ½ teaspoon ground mustard
- 1 teaspoon salt
- 1½ teaspoon pepper
- ½ teaspoon smoked paprika
- 1 tablespoon canola oil
- ¼ cup chicken stock
- 4 slices cooked bacon, crumbled

Directions:

1. In a small saucepan combine bourbon, sugar, garlic, vinegar, maple syrup, worcestershire and mustard. Bring to a boil, stirring constantly, then reduce heat to a simmer and let cook for 10-12 minutes, stirring occasionally. Remove from heat to thicken.
2. Preheat the grill to 350°F using direct heat with a cast iron grate installed.
3. Tenderize pork chops with a meat tenderizer, then coat on both sides with salt, pepper and paprika. Heat a cast iron griddle on the kamado grill and brush with canola oil and add pork chops. Sear on one side for 2 to 3 minutes; turn and cook for 2 to 3 minutes more. Slowly pour chicken stock over the chops, close bottom and top vents, and let the chops cook for about 10 minutes, until desired temperature is reached.
4. Once finished, pour glaze over top, add crumbled bacon and serve immediately.

BURGERS

Breakfast Burger

Servings: 4
Cooking Time: 13 Minutes

Ingredients:
- 1 1/2 lb ground beef
- 1/2 lb ground pork breakfast sausage
- 2 Tablespoon butter
- 8 strips bacon
- 4 slices sharp cheddar cheese
- 4 Brioche buns
- 4 eggs
- 4 thick slices tomato

Directions:
1. In a medium bowl, mix ground beef and sausage until just combined.
2. Form into 4 patties and refrigerate while the grill heats.
3. Melt butter in a large skillet and fry the eggs for 2 minutes on each side.
4. Grilling:
5. Preheat the grill to 400°F using direct heat with a cast iron grate installed.
6. Place bacon on a small cookie sheet and place on the grid in the grill. Cook until crispy.
7. Place the patties on the grid and close the dome for 3 minutes.
8. Flip the burgers and replace the dome for an additional 3 minutes.
9. Close all of the vents and allow the burgers to sit for an additional 5 minutes. The internal temperature of the burger should be 150°F.
10. Place cheese on top of the burgers and cover for 1 more minute.
11. Assemble the burgers by placing a burger on the bottom bun, topping with bacon, tomato, and a fried egg.

Classic American Burger

Servings: 4
Cooking Time: 12 Minutes

Ingredients:

- 2 lbs ground beef
- 1/2 tsp salt
- 1/4 tsp pepper
- 4 slices American cheese
- 4 hamburger buns
- Green Leaf Lettuce
- Sliced Tomato
- Ketchup
- Mustard
- Sliced Pickle

Directions:

1. Form ground beef into four patties and season both sides with salt and pepper.
2. Grilling:
3. Preheat the grill to 500°F using direct heat with a cast iron grate installed.
4. Place burgers on the grid and close the dome for 3 minutes.
5. Flip burgers and close the dome for 2 more minutes.
6. Close all of the vents and allow the burgers to sit for 5 minutes.
7. Top each burger with a slice of cheese and close the dome for 1 more minute.
8. Build burgers with lettuce, tomato, pickle, mustard, and ketchup.

Oahu Burger

Servings: 4
Cooking Time: 12 Minutes

Ingredients:

- 2 lbs ground beef
- 1/4 cup thickened Teriyaki Marinade
- 1/4 cup mayonnaise
- 1/2 tsp sambal or sriracha
- 4 slices fresh pineapple, cored
- 4 slices tomato
- 4 slices butter lettuce
- 4 Hawaiian hamburger buns

Directions:

1. Form ground beef into four patties and season both sides with salt and pepper.
2. In a small bowl, mix mayonnaise with hot chile sauce and spread on buns.
3. Top each bun with a burger, slice of pineapple, lettuce and tomato.
4. Grilling:
5. Preheat the grill to 500°F using direct heat with a cast iron grate installed.
6. Place burgers on the grid and close the dome for 3 minutes.
7. Flip burgers, baste with Teriyaki Marinade, and place the pineapple slices on the grid. Close the dome for 2 more minutes.
8. Flip the burgers again and baste with remaining Teriyaki Marinade. Close the dome.
9. Close all of the vents and allow the burgers to sit for 5 minutes.

Quesadilla Burger

Servings: 4
Cooking Time: 12 Minutes

Ingredients:

- 2 lbs ground beef
- 2 Tablespoons Adobo Rub
- 1 cup shredded cheddar cheese
- 4 large flour tortillas
- Sour Cream
- Guacamole
- Salsa

Directions:

1. Form ground beef into four patties and season both sides with Adobo Rub.
2. Serve each burger with sour cream, guacamole, and salsa.
3. Grilling:
4. Preheat the grill to 500°F using direct heat with a cast iron grate installed.
5. Place burgers on the grid and close the dome for 3 minutes.
6. Flip burgers and close the dome for 2 more minutes.
7. Close all of the vents and allow the burgers to sit for 5 minutes.
8. Remove burgers and place flour tortillas on the grid.
9. Top each tortilla with shredded cheese and close the dome for 1 minute until the cheese melts.
10. Place a hamburger in the center of each tortilla and begin folding the tortilla around the burger like an envelope.

The Crowned Jewels Burger

Servings: 4
Cooking Time: 12 Minutes

Ingredients:

- 2 lbs ground beef
- 1/2 tsp salt
- 1/4 tsp pepper
- 1 lb thinly sliced pastrami
- 1 cup shredded Romaine lettuce
- 1/4 cup mayonnaise
- 2 Tablespoons ketchup
- 1/8 tsp onion powder
- 4 slices Sharp Cheddar cheese
- 4 hamburger buns
- 1 tomato, sliced

Directions:

1. Form ground beef into four patties and season both sides with salt and pepper.
2. Meanwhile, mix together mayonnaise, ketchup, and onion powder. Smear on each bun.
3. Place each pastrami and cheese covered burger on the prepared buns and top with shredded lettuce and tomato.
4. Grilling:
5. Preheat the grill to 500°F using direct heat with a cast iron grate installed.
6. Place burgers on the grid and close the dome for 3 minutes.
7. Flip burgers and close the dome for 2 more minutes.
8. Close all of the vents and allow the burgers to sit for 5 minutes.
9. Top each burger with 1/4 of the pastrami and a slice of cheese and close the dome for 1 more minute.

"the Masterpiece"

Servings: 4
Cooking Time: 12 Minutes

Ingredients:

- 2 lbs ground beef
- 6 ounces sliced mushrooms
- 4 Tablespoons shredded smoked Gouda
- 2 Tablespoons butter
- 2 Tablespoons olive oil
- 2 Tablespoons Dijon mustard
- 1/2 tsp salt
- 1/4 tsp pepper
- 8 slices bacon, cooked and crumbled
- 4 slices Swiss cheese
- 4 brioche buns
- 1 small onion, sliced

Directions:

1. Heat a skillet over medium heat and add 1 Tablespoon butter and 1 Tablespoon olive oil.
2. Place mushrooms in the pan and DO NOT MOVE THEM. Saute for 5-7 minutes or until the mushrooms are browned. Remove from the pan and set aside.
3. In the same skillet, heat remaining butter and olive oil and add onions. Saute over medium heat until they become translucent and begin to brown, about 10 minutes. Remove from the heat and set aside to cool.
4. Mix onion, mushrooms, and crumbled bacon.
5. Grilling:
6. Preheat the grill to 425°F using direct heat with a cast iron grate installed.
7. Form ground beef into eight patties and season both sides with salt and pepper.
8. Place a generous spoonful of the mushroom and onion mixture in the center of four patties and top with smoked Gouda.
9. Top with additional patty and press sides to seal the mixture inside.
10. Place burgers on the grid and close the dome for 5 minutes.
11. Flip burgers and close the dome for 3 more minutes.
12. Close all of the vents and allow the burgers to sit for 5 minutes.
13. Top each burger with a slice of Swiss cheese and close the dome for 1 more minute.
14. Spread buns with mustard, top with burgers and bun tops.

DESSERTS

Apple Cake

Servings: 12
Cooking Time: 60 Minutes

Ingredients:

- 2 (21 oz) cans apple pie filling
- 1 (14 oz) jar caramel ice cream topping
- 1 box yellow cake mix, prepared according to package directions and mixed with 2 tsp cinnamon

Directions:

1. Prepare cake according to package directions.
2. Line a dutch oven with a liner.
3. Pour pie filling into the bottom of the dutch oven.
4. Top with caramel ice cream topping.
5. Top with prepared cake mix.
6. Grilling:
7. Preheat the grill to 350°F using direct heat with a cast iron grate installed.
8. Cover the dutch oven and place on the grid of the grill.
9. Lower the dome and cook for 1 hour.
10. Serve warm with whipped cream or ice cream.

Buttermilk Biscuits

Servings: 6
Cooking Time: 15 Minutes

Ingredients:

- 3/4 cups buttermilk
- 1/2 cup butter, cut into 1/2 inch cubes
- 3 cups flour
- 1 1/2 tsp baking powder
- 1/2 tsp salt

Directions:

1. In the bowl of a food processor, combine flour, baking powder, salt and butter and pulse until the butter is the size of small peas.
2. With the food processor going, stream in buttermilk until the dough just comes together.
3. Turn out on a floured surface.
4. Pat the dough to 1/2-inch thickness and fold in half.
5. Pat the dough to 1/2-inch thickness and fold in half again.
6. Pat the dough a third time to 1/2-inch thickness.
7. Using a pizza cutter, cut the dough into 12 square biscuits.
8. Place a sheet of parchment in the bottom of the dutch oven.
9. Place biscuits on the bottom of the dutch oven, being careful that they do not touch. (You may have to do this in two batches.)
10. Grilling:
11. Preheat the grill to 425°F using direct heat with a cast iron grate installed.
12. Cover the dutch oven with the lid and place on the grid.
13. Lower the dome for 12-15 minutes.
14. Biscuits are done when they are golden brown. Serve with butter, honey, or jam.

Best Banana Bread

Servings: 6
Cooking Time: 40 Minutes

Ingredients:

- 1 cup plain yogurt
- 1/4 cup butter
- 3 very ripe bananas, peeled
- 2 eggs
- 2 cups flour
- 2/3 cups sugar
- 3/4 tsp salt
- 1/2 tsp vanilla extract
- 1/2 tsp baking soda
- 1/4 tsp baking powder

Directions:

1. In a blender, combine bananas, yogurt, sugar, butter, vanilla, and eggs until smooth.
2. In a large bowl, sift together flour, salt, baking powder, and baking soda.
3. Gradually add the wet ingredients into the dry ingredients and gently stir to combine. DO NOT OVER MIX.
4. Line a dutch oven with a liner.
5. Pour batter into the dutch oven and cover.
6. Grilling:
7. Preheat the grill to 350°F using direct heat with a cast iron grate installed and place the dutch oven on the grid.
8. Lower the dome for 30 minutes or until a toothpick inserted into the center comes out clean.

Peanut Butter Bacon Bars

Servings: 8
Cooking Time: 25 Minutes

Ingredients:

- 1 package peanut butter cookie mix
- 1/2 cup chopped peanuts
- 1/2 cup bacon, cooked and crumbled
- 1/3 cup vegetable oil
- 1 egg
- 1 cup semi-sweet chocolate chips
- 1/2 cup bacon, cooked and crumbled

Directions:

1. Combine cookie mix, vegetable oil, egg, bacon, and peanuts and press into a lined dutch oven.
2. Grilling:
3. Preheat the grill to 350°F using direct heat with a cast iron grate installed.
4. Cover the dutch oven and place on the grid.
5. Lower the dome for 25 minutes.
6. Remove the lid and top with chocolate chips.
7. Replace the cover for 5 minutes until the chocolate chips are melted.
8. Spread the chocolate over the bars to coat them evenly.
9. Top with remaining bacon.
10. Allow the bars to cool before cutting.

4 Ingredient, No Knead Bread

Servings: 4
Cooking Time: 30 Minutes

Ingredients:

- 3 cups warm water
- 1 1/2 Tablespoons yeast
- 1 1/2 Tablespoons salt
- 6 1/2 cups bread flour

Directions:

1. In a 4-quart ice cream container, mix all ingredients until they come together. DO NOT KNEAD.
2. Cover, but do not seal the container and allow it to sit in a warm, dry place until it doubles in size, about 30 minutes.
3. Seal the container and place in the fridge for 1 hour.
4. Place a sheet of parchment paper in the bottom of the dutch oven.
5. Pinch off 1/4 of the dough and form into a ball.
6. Place the ball on the parchment paper and allow it to rest while the grill heats.
7. Grilling:
8. Preheat the grill to 425°F using direct heat with a cast iron grate installed.
9. Score the top of the dough ball with an "X".
10. Cover the dutch oven and place it on the grid of the grill.
11. Lower the Dome for 30 minutes.
12. Remove the bread from the dutch oven and allow it to cool before slicing.

Almond Cream Cake

Servings: 16
Cooking Time: 45 Minutes

Ingredients:

- 2 cups butter, softened
- 3 cups sugar
- 6 cups cake flour
- 1 tsp kosher salt
- 4 tsp baking powder
- 2 cups whole milk
- 2 tsp almond extract
- 10 large eggs, whites only
- sliced almonds, to decorate
- for the frosting
- 11⁄4 cups all-purpose flour
- 2 cups whole milk
- 1⁄2 tsp almond extract
- 1 tbsp vanilla bean paste
- 2 cups butter, softened
- 2 cups sugar

Directions:

1. In the bowl of a stand mixer fitted with the paddle attachment, cream butter until white in appearance. Add sugar and beat until fluffy. In a large bowl, sift together flour, salt, and baking powder. Add the flour mixture to the butter mixture in three stages, alternating with the milk and almond extract and mixing after each addition until just combined.
2. In a large bowl, beat egg whites until they form stiff peaks. Using a spatula, gently fold egg whites into the cake batter, taking care not to overmix.
3. Preheat the grill to 350°F (177°C) using indirect heat with a standard grate installed. Line an11 x18-in (28 x 46cm) grill-safe baking pan with parchment paper and lightly grease with cooking spray. Pour the batter into the pan, place on the grate, close the lid, and bake until the top springs back when touched, about 27 to 30 minutes.
4. Remove the cake from the grill and place on a wire rack to cool for 10 minutes. Use a knife to loosen the edges, and transfer the cake to a wire rack to cool completely.
5. To make the frosting, on the stovetop in a saucepan over medium-low heat, whisk together flour and milk until mixture thickens to the consistency of mashed potatoes, about 12 to 15 minutes. Stir constantly, and lower the heat if needed. Remove the saucepan from the heat and place in a bowl of ice for 5 to 10 minutes to hasten the cooling process and bring the mixture to room temperature. Once cool, stir in almond extract.
6. In the bowl of a stand mixer, cream together vanilla paste, butter, and sugar until the mixture is light and fluffy and sugar is completely dissolved. Add the flour mixture, and beat until it has the appearance of whipped cream, scraping the sides of the bowl as needed.
7. Spread the frosting evenly over the cooled cake and sprinkle sliced almonds over top to decorate before serving.

Corn & Jalapeño Focaccia

Servings: 8
Cooking Time: 40 Minutes

Ingredients:

- 21⁄2 cups all-purpose or bread flour
- 1 tbsp kosher salt
- 1⁄2 tbsp instant dry yeast
- 11⁄2 cups warm water (105°F [41°C])
- 3 tbsp extra virgin olive oil
- 3 jalapeño peppers, left whole
- 1 ear of corn, shucked
- for the butter
- 1 tbsp olive oil
- 2 tbsp unsalted butter
- 4 garlic cloves, minced
- 2 tsp dried oregano
- 1⁄2 tsp red pepper flakes
- kosher salt

Directions:

1. In a large bowl, combine flour, salt, yeast, and water. Cover tightly with plastic wrap, and set aside to rest for at least 8 hours and up to 24 hours. The dough will rise dramatically and fill the bowl.
2. Pour oil into a large cast iron skillet. Transfer the dough to the skillet, turning the dough to coat in oil. Press the dough around the skillet, flattening slightly and spreading to fill the entire bottom. Cover tightly with plastic wrap and let sit at room temperature for 2 hours.
3. After the first hour, preheat the grill to 425°F (218°C) using indirect heat with a standard grate installed. Place jalapeños and corn on the grate near the edges. Close the lid and grill until beginning to soften and char, about 10 to 12 minutes. Cut the kernels from the cob, and seed and dice jalapeños. Set aside.
4. After resting for 2 hours, the dough should mostly fill the skillet. Use your fingertips to firmly press the dough to the edges, popping any large bubbles that appear. Lift the dough at the edges and allow any air bubbles underneath to escape.
5. Evenly scatter corn and jalapeños over the dough, then push down until they're embedded in the dough. Place the skillet on the grate, close the grill lid, and bake until the top is golden brown and the bottom appears golden brown and crisp when lifted at the edge with a spatula, about 16 to 24 minutes.
6. To make the butter, on the stovetop in a small saucepan over medium-low heat, heat oil and butter until butter melts. Add garlic, oregano, and pepper flakes, and cook for 1 minute, stirring constantly. Transfer to a small bowl and season with salt to taste.
7. Transfer the focaccia to a cutting board and brush the butter over top. Allow to cool slightly, slice, and serve with any remaining butter.

S'mores Pizza

Servings: 8
Cooking Time: 5 Minutes

Ingredients:

- 1 pizza dough
- 1/2 cup semi-sweet chocolate chips
- 1/2 cup miniature marshmallows
- 1/4 cup slightly crushed graham crackers

Directions:

1. Stretch dough to a 14" round and place on a pizza peel.
2. Sprinkle dough with chocolate chips, miniature marshmallows, and graham cracker crumbs.
3. Grilling:
4. Slide the pizza onto the prepared stone at 500°F.
5. Cook for 5 minutes, remove from the stone, slice, and serve.

Grilled Watermelon With Honey Yogurt

Servings: 4
Cooking Time: 4 Minutes

Ingredients:

- 1 round of watermelon, 1 inch thick
- 1/2 cup Greek-style yogurt
- 1 Tablespoon honey
- 1/4 tsp vanilla

Directions:

1. Place the watermelon on a 400°F grill with the dome down for 1 minute.
2. Turn the watermelon and lower the dome for an additional minute.
3. Assembly:
4. Cut the watermelon in quarters and place each on a small plate.
5. In a small bowl, combine yogurt, honey, and vanilla and spoon equal amounts over the watermelon. Serve.

Bread Pudding

Servings: 8
Cooking Time: 60 Minutes

Ingredients:

- 1 1/2 cups milk
- 10 eggs
- 1 loaf French bread, cut into 1 1/2 inch cubes
- 1 1/2 cups sugar
- 1 cup raisins (optional)
- 2 Tablespoons vanilla
- 2 tsp cinnamon
- 1/2 tsp nutmeg
- 1/4 tsp salt

Directions:

1. Line the dutch oven with a liner.
2. Place bread cubes and raisins into the dutch oven.
3. In a large bowl, combine eggs, milk, sugar, vanilla, cinnamon, nutmeg, and salt.
4. Pour the mixture over the bread and raisins.
5. Allow the bread mixture to sit for 30 minutes.
6. Grilling:
7. Preheat the grill to 350°F using direct heat with a cast iron grate installed.
8. Cover the dutch oven, place it on the grid, and lower the dome for 1 hour.
9. Serve the bread pudding with vanilla ice cream or whipped cream.

Grilled Fruit Pie

Servings: 8
Cooking Time: 55 Minutes

Ingredients:

- for the crust
- 1 cup all-purpose flour, plus extra for rolling dough
- 1⁄2 tsp kosher salt
- 1⁄2 cup butter, chilled and cut into small cubes
- 1⁄4 cup ice water
- 2lb (1kg) dried beans, for blind baking
- powdered sugar, for dusting
- whipped cream or ice cream, to serve (optional)
- for the filling
- 11⁄4lb (565g) seasonal fruit, such as pears and plums, halved and pitted
- 1⁄2 cup sugar
- 4 tbsp cornstarch
- 2 tbsp lemon juice

Directions:

1. Preheat the grill to 350°F (177°C) using indirect heat with a standard grate installed. Place fruit on the grate skin side up, keeping them toward the edges of the grate. Close the lid and grill until beginning to soften, about 3 to 5 minutes. Transfer to a cutting board and slice. Set aside.
2. To make the crust, in a food processor, combine flour and salt, pulsing 3 to 4 times. Add butter, and pulse until the texture is mealy, about 5 to 6 times. With the food processor running, slowly add the ice water in 1 tbsp increments until the dough comes together.
3. Turn out the dough onto a floured work surface and sprinkle with flour. Using a rolling pin, roll dough out to a 10- to 11-in (25- to 28-cm) circle. Carefully transfer the dough to a 9-in (23-cm) metal pie pan, pressing the dough to the edges. Trim any overhang and crimp the edges. Prick the dough with a fork to prevent bubbles during baking. Place the pan in the fridge to chill for 15 minutes.
4. Spread a large piece of parchment paper over the dough and fill the pan with dry beans, pressing them into the edges of the dough. Place the pan on the grate, close the lid, and bake for 10 minutes. Remove the parchment and beans from the pan, and continue baking the crust until golden brown in color, about 10 to 15 minutes more. Remove the pan from the grill and let the crust cool completely before filling.
5. To make the filling, in a large bowl, combine sugar, cornstarch, and juice. Add the grilled fruit and toss lightly to coat. Pour the fruit mixture into the baked crust. Place on the grate, close the lid, and bake until the filling is thickened and bubbling at the edges, about 30 minutes.
6. Remove the pie from the grill and place on a wire rack to cool. Just before serving, sprinkle with powdered sugar. Serve with whipped cream or ice cream (if desired).

Berry Upside-down Cake

Servings: 10
Cooking Time: 30 Minutes

Ingredients:

- 10 tbsp unsalted butter, at room temperature, divided
- 1 cup packed light brown sugar, divided
- 11oz (315g) fresh seasonal berries
- 1 large egg
- 1 tsp pure vanilla extract
- 2⁄3 cup sour cream
- 11⁄3 cups all-purpose flour
- 1 tbsp baking powder
- 1⁄4 tsp baking soda
- 1⁄2 tsp kosher salt
- 1⁄4 tsp ground cinnamon
- fresh mint leaves, to garnish
- whipped cream, to serve

Directions:

1. Preheat the grill to 350°F (177°C) using indirect heat with a standard grate installed and a cast iron skillet on the grate. Melt 2 tbsp butter in the skillet and swirl to coat. Remove the skillet from the grill. Sprinkle 1⁄3 cup brown sugar over butter, pour in berries, and shake the skillet until berries are evenly spread out. Set aside.
2. In the bowl of a stand mixer fitted with the paddle attachment, cream together remaining 8 tbsp butter and 2⁄3 cup brown sugar until fluffy. Add egg, vanilla, and sour cream, and beat to combine.
3. In a medium bowl, sift together flour, baking powder, baking soda, salt, and cinnamon. Gradually add the dry ingredients to the butter and egg mixture until just incorporated. (The batter will be thick.) Using a rubber spatula, scoop the batter into the skillet, smoothing it over berries.
4. Place the skillet on the grate, close the lid, and bake until golden brown and a cake tester inserted into the middle of the cake comes out clean, about 30 minutes. Remove the skillet from the grill and place on a wire rack to cool for 15 minutes.
5. To serve, flip the cake upside down on a large serving platter and release from the skillet, leaving the berries on top. Garnish with fresh mint leaves, and serve with a dollop of whipped cream.

Apple Pizza

Servings: 8
Cooking Time: 5 Minutes

Ingredients:

- 1 pizza dough
- 1 cup apple pie filling
- 1/4 cup vanilla cake mix
- 2 Tablespoon melted butter
- Vanilla Ice Cream

Directions:

1. Stretch pizza dough into a 14" round and place on a pizza peel.
2. In a small bowl, combine cake mix and melted butter until it forms a crumbly texture.
3. Spread apple pie filling over pizza dough and top with crumb mixture.
4. Grilling:
5. Bake on a pizza stone in a 500°F grill for 5 minutes.
6. Slice and serve with vanilla frosting.

3 Ingredient Fruit Cobbler

Servings: 8
Cooking Time: 30 Minutes

Ingredients:

- 1 stick butter, sliced
- 2 (29 oz) cans fruit, drained but reserving 1/2 cup of the liquid
- 1 yellow cake mix

Directions:

1. Line the dutch oven with a liner
2. Pour fruit into the bottom of the dutch oven with 1/2 cup of reserved liquid
3. Sprinkle the top with cake mix
4. Dot the top with butter.
5. Grilling:
6. Preheat the grill to 350°F using direct heat with a cast iron grate installed.
7. Cover the dutch oven and place on the grid of the grill.
8. Lower the dome for 30 minutes.
9. Allow the cobbler to sit for 10 minutes off the heat before serving.

SIDES

Grilled Caesar Salad

Servings: 6
Cooking Time: 1 Minutes

Ingredients:

- 2 Tablespoons shredded Parmesan cheese
- 1 Tablespoon olive oil
- 1/4 tsp salt
- 2 heads romaine lettuce, split lengthwise
- 1 cup grated Parmesan cheese
- 2 Tablespoons Dijon mustard
- 3 garlic cloves
- 3 anchovy fillets
- 2 lemons, juiced
- Extra-virgin olive oil
- Kosher salt
- 2 Tablespoons olive oil
- 4 slices day old Italian bread, cubed
- Kosher Salt & Black Pepper to taste

Directions:

1. In a blender or food processor, combine dressing ingredients, minus olive oil and salt.
2. Gradually stream in olive oil until the dressing reaches your desired consistency.
3. Taste and season with salt, if necessary.
4. Grilling:
5. Preheat the grill to 400°F using direct heat with a cast iron grate installed.
6. Toss bread cubes with olive oil, a pinch of salt and a pinch of black pepper and place on a small sheet tray.
7. Place the bread in the grill for 8-10 minutes or until golden brown.
8. Brush cut side of the romaine halves with olive oil and season with salt and pepper.
9. Grill 1 minute over direct heat.
10. Cut the romaine into bite size pieces.
11. Toss lettuce with dressing, croutons, and shredded Parmesan Serve immediately.

Sweet Potato Fries

Servings: 4
Cooking Time: 25 Minutes

Ingredients:

- 1 tsp fresh thyme, chopped
- 4 large sweet potatoes
- 4 cloves garlic, minced
- 1/4 cup olive oil
- Salt and Pepper

Directions:

1. In a large pot, cover sweet potatoes with cold water and add 2 tsp salt.
2. Bring the water to a boil and cook until the potatoes are soft, but firm, about 15 minutes.
3. In a small sauce pan, heat 2 Tablespoon of the olive oil, garlic, and thyme until fragrant.
4. Cut each sweet potato in half, lengthwise, then in 3 or 4 spears.
5. Brush each spear on cut sides with olive oil, season with salt and pepper.
6. Grilling:
7. Preheat the grill to 425°F using direct heat with a cast iron grate installed and close the dome for 3 minutes.
8. Turn the potatoes and close the dome for an additional 3 minutes or until the sweet potatoes have finished cooking through.
9. Remove the fries and toss with the garlic and thyme oil before serving.

Grilled Sweet Potatoes

Servings: 12
Cooking Time: 20 Minutes

Ingredients:

- 5 tbsp olive oil
- 5 tbsp pure maple syrup
- 3 tbsp kosher salt
- 6 garlic cloves, minced, plus more to serve
- 2 tsp finely chopped fresh thyme leaves
- 1⁄4 tsp crushed red pepper flakes
- 6 large sweet potatoes, about 3lb (1.4kg) in total, peeled and cut into thick wedges
- 2 tbsp finely chopped fresh flat-leaf parsley

Directions:

1. Preheat the grill to 400°F using direct heat with a cast iron grate installed.
2. In a large bowl, whisk together oil, syrup, salt, garlic, thyme, and red pepper flakes. Add potatoes and toss to coat. Season with more salt (if desired).
3. Place wedges on the grate, being sure to shake off excess liquid, close the lid, and grill until lightly golden brown and just cooked through, about 15 to 20 minutes, turning often.
4. Transfer to a serving bowl and immediately toss with parsley and more minced garlic (if desired). Season with salt to taste.

Alligator Eggs

Servings: 6
Cooking Time: 10 Minutes

Ingredients:

- 8 ounces cream cheese, softened
- 1 cup sharp cheddar cheese
- 12 thin slices bacon
- 6 jalapeños

Directions:

1. Slice jalapeños in half and remove seeds. Set aside.
2. In a small bowl, combine cheddar cheese and cream cheese until mixed.
3. Stuff 2 Tablespoon of the cream cheese mixture into each jalapeño half.
4. Wrap each jalapeño half in one strip of bacon, securing with a toothpick.
5. Grilling:
6. Preheat the grill to 425°F using direct heat with a cast iron grate installed.
7. Place the alligator eggs directly on the grid and close the dome for 10 minutes or until the bacon is crisp. Serve immediately.

Mexican Street Corn

Servings: 6
Cooking Time: 10 Minutes

Ingredients:

- 6 ears corn
- 1/2 cup cotija cheese
- 1 Tablespoon chili powder
- 1 cup mayonnaise
- 1 lime, cut into wedges

Directions:

1. Pull back the husk of the corn and thoroughly remove the silk from each ear of corn.
2. Soak the corn in water for 20 minutes before cooking.
3. Peel back the husks to reveal the corn.
4. Grilling:
5. Preheat the grill to 450°F using direct heat with a cast iron grate installed.
6. Close the dome for 5 minutes, turn the corn, and close the dome for an additional 5 minutes.
7. Remove the corn from the grill. Spread with mayonnaise, sprinkle with chili powder, and coat with cotija cheese.
8. Serve with lime wedges.

Wood-plank Loaded Mashed Potatoes

Servings: 16
Cooking Time: 50 Minutes

Ingredients:

- 1lb (450g) red potatoes
- 1lb (450g) Yukon Gold potatoes
- 1 tbsp kosher salt, plus 1 tsp
- 2 strips bacon, diced
- 2 tbsp unsalted butter
- 1⁄4 cup sour cream
- 1⁄4 cup heavy cream
- 4oz (113g) shredded Cheddar cheese, plus more for topping
- 4 scallions, thinly sliced, plus more for topping
- freshly ground black pepper

Directions:

1. Place a 4 x 9in (10 x 23cm) cedar wood plank in a baking dish, cover with cold water, and place heavy cans or stones on the plank to keep it submerged. Soak for 1 to 2 hours.
2. Place red potatoes and Yukon Gold potatoes in a large stockpot and add cold water to cover by several inches. Place the pot on the stovetop over high heat, add 1 tsp salt, and bring to a boil. Reduce to a simmer, cover, and cook until potatoes are fork tender, about 25 minutes. Drain potatoes, reserving 1 cup cooking water.
3. Preheat the grill to 350°F (177°C) using direct heat with a standard grate installed and a cast iron skillet on the grate. Add bacon to the hot skillet, and cook until bacon is crisp and the fat has rendered, about 10 to 15 minutes, stirring occasionally. Transfer the cooked bacon pieces to a plate lined with a paper towel.
4. In a large bowl, combine potatoes, butter, sour cream, heavy cream, Cheddar cheese, scallions, bacon, and 1 tbsp salt. Mash with a potato masher until potatoes have broken down and cheese and sour cream are fully incorporated. If potatoes are too stiff, add some of the reserved cooking water.
5. Place the soaked plank on the grate and allow it to heat for 2 to 5 minutes, then flip it over. Scoop the mashed potatoes onto the heated side of the plank. Top the potatoes with a little Cheddar cheese, close the lid, and cook until cheese has melted and potatoes have browned slightly, about 7 to 10 minutes. Remove potatoes from the grill, sprinkle with scallions, and serve immediately.

Grilled Vegetable Succotash

Servings: 6
Cooking Time: 10 Minutes

Ingredients:

- 3 ears corn, shucked and cleaned
- 1 (9 ounces) package baby lima beans, thawed and rinsed
- 1 large tomato, diced
- 1 zucchini, cut lengthwise into 1/2 inch thick slices
- 1 jalapeño
- Additional olive oil for brushing
- 1/3 cup olive oil
- 1/2 tsp salt
- 1/2 tsp pepper
- 1/4 tsp cumin
- The juice of 2 limes

Directions:

1. Grilling:
2. Brush the corn and zucchini on all sides with olive oil.
3. Place the corn on a 500°F grill and lower the dome for 5 minutes.
4. Turn the corn, place the zucchini on the grill, and lower the dome for an additional 5 minutes.
5. Remove the corn, turn the zucchini and cook for 1 minute more.
6. Assembly:
7. Remove the corn from the cob and dice the cooked zucchini.
8. In a large bowl, combine dressing ingredients.
9. Add lima beans, corn, zucchini, tomato, and jalapeño to the bowl and stir to combine.
10. Serve at room temperature.

Breakfast Casserole

Servings: 6
Cooking Time: 40 Minutes

Ingredients:

- 1 lb bulk pork breakfast sausage
- 1 (16 oz) bag of frozen O'Brien style hash browns
- 1 dozen eggs, beaten
- 1/4 cup grated onion
- 1/4 tsp black pepper
- Hot sauce for garnish

Directions:

1. Preheat the grill to 350°F using direct heat with a cast iron grate installed with the dutch oven on the grid.
2. Brown sausage with onion in the dutch oven.
3. Add hash browns and stir to combine.
4. Add eggs and cover.
5. Lower the dome for 15 minutes or until the eggs are just cooked through.
6. Serve the casserole with hot sauce for garnish.

Potato, Squash, And Tomato Gratin

Servings: 8
Cooking Time: 35 Minutes

Ingredients:

- 1 lb Yukon gold potatoes, sliced 1/4 inch thick
- 1 lb yellow squash, sliced 1/4 inch thick
- 1/2 cup shredded parmesan cheese
- 5 tomatoes, sliced 1/4 inch thick
- 1/4 cup olive oil, divided
- 2 Tablespoons garlic, minced
- 1 tsp salt
- 1/2 tsp pepper

Directions:

1. Line the bottom of the dutch oven with 2 Tablespoon olive oil.
2. Layer potatoes on the bottom, topped with squash, and topped with tomatoes.
3. Season the tomatoes with salt, pepper, half of the garlic, and half of the parmesan cheese.
4. Repeat with remaining potatoes, squash, and tomatoes.
5. Season with salt, pepper, and remaining garlic.
6. Drizzle with remaining 2 Tablespoon of olive oil and top with remaining parmesan cheese.
7. Grilling:
8. Preheat the grill to 375°F using direct heat with a cast iron grate installed.
9. Place the dutch oven, uncovered, into the grill and close the dome for 30-35 minutes or until the potatoes are cooked through.

Grilled Vegetable & Couscous Salad

Servings: 6
Cooking Time: 30 Minutes

Ingredients:

- 1 small zucchini, halved
- 1 small yellow squash, halved
- 1/2 red onion
- 6 sun-dried tomatoes
- 1 tbsp olive oil
- 2 cups uncooked Israeli couscous
- 4 cups vegetable stock, heated
- 4 basil leaves, stacked, rolled, and cut crosswise into thin strips, plus more to garnish
- 2 tbsp coarsely chopped fresh flat-leaf parsley, plus more to garnish
- for the marinade
- 1/4 cup balsamic vinegar
- 1/2 tsp Dijon mustard
- 1 garlic clove, coarsely chopped
- 1/2 cup olive oil
- kosher salt and freshly ground black pepper

Directions:

1. To make the marinade, in a small bowl, whisk together vinegar, mustard, and garlic. Slowly add oil, whisking until combined. Season with salt and pepper to taste.
2. Place zucchini, yellow squash, onion, and sun-dried tomatoes in a shallow dish. Pour half the marinade over the vegetables, toss to coat, and let sit at room temperature for 15 minutes. Cover the remaining marinade and set aside.
3. Preheat the grill to 400°F (204°C) with a cast iron grate installed and a dutch oven on the grate. Remove the vegetables from the marinade and place on the grate around the dutch oven. Close the lid and grill until beginning to soften and char, about 7 to 10 minutes. Transfer the vegetables to a cutting board and cut into bite-sized pieces. Set aside.
4. In the hot dutch oven, heat oil until shimmering. Add couscous, and toast until lightly golden brown, about 2 minutes. Add vegetable stock until couscous is just covered (add hot water if more liquid is needed to cover), close the grill lid, and bring to a boil. Cook until firm to the bite, about 7 to 10 minutes, and drain well.
5. Spoon the couscous into a large serving bowl and add the grilled vegetables, basil, and parsley. Drizzle the reserved marinade over top, and toss well to coat. Serve at room temperature with more basil and parsley to garnish.

Arroz A La Mexicana (mexican Rice)

Servings: 8
Cooking Time: 30 Minutes

Ingredients:

- 2 small white onions, peeled and halved
- 2 poblano peppers, left whole
- 2 carrots, peeled
- 1⁄4 cup vegetable oil
- 3 garlic cloves, minced
- 2 cups uncooked white rice
- 4 cups chicken stock
- 1⁄4 cup tomato paste
- 11⁄2 tbsp ground cumin
- 1 bunch of fresh cilantro, chopped

Directions:

1. Preheat the grill to 400°F (204°C) using direct heat with a cast iron grate installed and a dutch oven on the grate. Place onions, peppers, and carrots on the grate around the dutch oven, close the lid, and grill until beginning to soften and char, about 7 to 10 minutes. Remove the vegetables from the grill, chop onions and peppers, and dice carrots into small cubes.
2. In the hot dutch oven, heat oil until shimmering. Add carrots, and cook for 2 minutes, stirring occasionally. Stir in onions and garlic, and cook for 1 minute, stirring occasionally. Add rice, stock, tomato paste, and cumin. Bring to a boil, stirring once or twice. Cover the dutch oven with its lid and close the grill lid. Cook until rice is tender and liquid is absorbed, about 15 minutes.
3. Remove the dutch oven from the grill, stir peppers and cilantro into the rice, and fluff the rice with a fork. Serve immediately.

Broiled Tomatoes And Parmesan

Servings: 4
Cooking Time: 5 Minutes

Ingredients:

- 1/4 cup parmesan, shredded
- 4 roma tomatoes
- 1 Tablespoon olive oil
- 1 tsp red wine vinegar
- Salt & Pepper

Directions:

1. Cut each tomato in half, lengthwise, and brush with olive oil.
2. Grilling:
3. Preheat the grill to 500°F using direct heat with a cast iron grate installed and lower the dome for 2 minutes.
4. Turn the tomatoes, season with vinegar, salt, and pepper and top with parmesan cheese.
5. Lower the dome for an additional 2 minutes or until the cheese melts. Serve warm.

Smoked Potato Salad

Servings: 8
Cooking Time: 120 Minutes

Ingredients:

- 4 large baking potatoes
- 4 large eggs, hard boiled and finely chopped
- 2 green onions, finely chopped
- 2 large dill pickles, finely chopped
- 1 rib celery, finely diced
- 1/2 cup mayonnaise
- The juice of 1 lemon
- 1/2 tsp black pepper
- 1/2 tsp celery seed
- 1/2 tsp dried dill

Directions:

1. Scrub the potatoes.
2. Grilling:
3. Place the potatoes alongside meat that is smoking at 225°F.
4. Assembly:
5. When the potatoes are fork tender, chill in the refrigerator for 30 minutes.
6. Peel and cut potatoes into small cubes.
7. In a large bowl, combine dressing ingredients.
8. Add potatoes, eggs, green onion, pickle, and celery to the dressing and gently toss

Grilled Lemon Garlic Zucchini

Servings: 6
Cooking Time: 5 Minutes

Ingredients:

- 4 zucchini, sliced lengthwise into 1/2 inch slices
- 1/4 cup butter, softened
- 2 tsp parsley, chopped
- 3 cloves garlic, minced
- The zest and juice of 1 lemon

Directions:

1. In a small dish, combine butter, parsley, garlic, lemon zest, and lemon juice.
2. Liberally brush each zucchini slice with the butter mixture.
3. Grilling:
4. Place the zucchini on a 500°F grill and close the dome for 3 minutes.
5. Flip the zucchini and recover with the dome for an additional 2 minutes.
6. Drizzle remaining butter on top of zucchini as it comes off the grill. Serve warm.

RECIPES INDEX

Printed in France by Amazon
Brétigny-sur-Orge, FR

16232123R00065